Publisher's Message for
FOOD SECURITY

To shed light on today's cultural, social, economic, and political issues that are shaping our future as Canadians, Dundurn's **Point of
View Books** offer readers the informed opinions of knowledgeable
individuals.

Whatever the topic, the author of a **Point of View** book is someone we've invited to address a vital topic because their front-line experience, arising from personal immersion in the issue, gives readers
an engaging perspective, even though a reader may not ultimately
reach all the same conclusions as the author.

Our publishing house is committed to framing the hard choices
facing Canadians in a way that will spur democratic debate in our
country. For over forty years, Dundurn has been "defining Canada
for Canadians." Now our **Point of View Books**, under the direction
of general editor J. Patrick Boyer, take us a further step on this journey of national discovery.

Each author of a **Point of View** book has an important message,
and a definite point of view about an issue close to their heart. Some
Point of View Books will resemble manifestos for action, others
will shed light on a crucial subject from an alternative perspective,
and a few will be concise statements of a timely case needing to be
clearly made.

But whatever the topic or whomever the author, all these titles
will be eye-openers for Canadians, engaging issues that matter to us
as citizens.

J. Kirk Howard
Publisher Emeritus
Dundurn Press

A Note from the General Editor

A decade ago, officials from China visiting Toronto to study advances in medicine were asked by Ontario's deputy minister of health about their country's public health program. "The only thing that kept Chairman Mao awake at night was worrying how to feed a billion people every day," came the response. "Our health policy is unchanged."

The problem that Mao wrestled with is faced by the whole world today. A century ago, fewer than two billion humans had to eat; today, more than seven billion do.

It's easy to see how all species share the dynamic relationship connecting available food and their population levels. Food's direct link with human history is also clear: Europeans learned of major new crops from America's Indigenous peoples, denying food has been a weapon in wartime, improvements in trade and transportation lead to changed diets.

It's more difficult, though, to get a handle on the future of food security. What do science and experience really teach about production, consumption, and population? Trend lines suggest very different possible futures: mean harvests and extinction; alternatively, abundant yields and well-being.

In his youth, Ralph Martin learned "the wisdom of agriculture" and got a handle on feeding humanity and honouring ecology. Today, as a professor at the University of Guelph, his work exemplifies the excellent scholarship of this world-leading centre for research into agricultural science and its practical application. As he engaged a Science for Peace audience about "Food Security," I envisaged this book and I'm grateful he's written it.

It is difficult to condense so much understanding about food and society. But what Ralph Martin encapsulated for a public talk, he's managed again in this timely work of global significance. His optimistic realism, as you will discover in this roadmap to tomorrow, finds the necessary balance for moving "from excess to enough."

J. Patrick Boyer
General Editor
Point of View Books

FOOD SECURITY

Other Point of View Titles

Irresponsible Government
by Brent Rathgeber
Foreword by Andrew Coyne

Time Bomb
by Douglas L. Bland
Foreword by Bonnie Butlin

Two Freedoms
by Hugh Segal
Foreword by Tom Axworthy

Off the Street
By W.A. Bogart
Foreword by Sukanya Pillay

Charlie Foxtrot
by Kim Richard Nossal
Foreword by Ferry de Kerckhove

Sir John's Echo
by John Boyko
Foreword by Lawrence Martin

Dynamic Forest
by Malcolm F. Squires
Foreword by John Kennedy Naysmith

Beyond Incarceration
by Paula Mallea
Foreword by Catherine Latimer

RALPH C. MARTIN

FOOD SECURITY

From Excess to Enough

Foreword by Elizabeth May

DUNDURN

A J. PATRICK BOYER BOOK

TORONTO

Publisher: Scott Fraser | Acquiring editor: J. Patrick Boyer | Editor: Dominic Farrell
Cover designer: Laura Boyle
Cover image: istock.com/elenabs
Printer: Webcom, a division of Marquis Book Printing Inc.

Library and Archives Canada Cataloguing in Publication

Title: Food security : from excess to enough / Ralph C. Martin ; foreword by Elizabeth May.
Names: Martin, Ralph C. (Ralph Cameron), 1953- author. | May, Elizabeth, writer of foreword.
Series: Point of view (Dundurn Press)
Description: Series statement: Point of view | "A J. Patrick Boyer book." | Includes bibliographical references.
Identifiers: Canadiana (print) 20190154233 | Canadiana (ebook) 20190154241 | ISBN 9781459744028 (softcover) | ISBN 9781459744035 (PDF) | ISBN 9781459744042 (EPUB)
Subjects: LCSH: Food consumption—Canada. | LCSH: Food supply—Canada. | LCSH: Food security—Canada. | LCSH: Agricultural industries—Canada. | LCSH: Agriculture—Environmental aspects—Canada.
Classification: LCC HD9014.C32 M37 2019 | DDC 338.1/971—dc23

We acknowledge the support of the Canada Council for the Arts and the Ontario Arts Council for our publishing program. We also acknowledge the financial support of the Government of Ontario, through the Ontario Book Publishing Tax Credit and Ontario Creates, and the Government of Canada.

Printed and bound in Canada.

VISIT US AT

 dundurn.com | @dundurnpress |  dundurnpress | dundurnpress

Dundurn
3 Church Street, Suite 500
Toronto, Ontario, Canada
M5E 1M2

Mariah patiently teaches me and my life is enriched.

CONTENTS

FOREWORD

Ralph Martin is someone I have respected for years. Back when I lived in Nova Scotia, his work promoting organic agriculture was groundbreaking. As a professor at the University of Guelph, he has continued and expanded the scope of his science and of his advocacy. This is an important book.

The book you hold in your hands defies neat categorization. Is it a text on the perils of the industrial agriculture model? A spiritual reflection on our consumer culture? A scientific review of how our appetite for stuff is overwhelming our living systems?

It is actually all three, and a bit more.

Food is obviously essential for life, but it provides more than sustenance for our physical bodies. The growing of it and the eating of it underpins and informs all of human culture. It provides powerful stuff for allegory. Humans are at the top of what we call "food chains." That's one way of looking at things. Woody Allen sees the food chain in another way. He says, "To me nature is … spiders and bugs, and big fish eating little fish, and plants eating plants, and animals eating.… It's like an enormous restaurant."

The earliest settled civilization began when the first primitive hoe struck the earth and cultivation began. Once we gave up a nomadic existence it was possible to start saving — hoarding.

Gardens are the stuff of myth and metaphor. Three of the main religions of the world — Judaism, Christianity, and Islam — share the same belief in how the world, and everything on it, was created. We humans were the last creatures created by God, formed after the solid mass was called forth from the void, after light was separated from dark, and so on. Finally, on the sixth day, two naked humans were placed into a garden. It's interesting that, according to the three religions mentioned, God did not place us in wild nature. The home created for humans was cultivated before we got there. Not for the three major religions the myth of humans emerging from a shell on a beach to squint at the sun, as the Haida believe. Or being formed in all the colours of the human race baked in clay in a desert, as the Hopi stories tell us. Not coming to a place where the sky was so close you could touch it and everyone had all they needed as in the Nigerian tales of the world's beginning. The Garden of Eden contained all that we could ever want. More than enough food, water, and shelter. That garden contained every animal on earth, but there were no threats to humans. No animals ate the flesh of other animals. And we were given one simple instruction — you can eat anything you want, except the fruit from that one tree.

We know how that went. Humans are not very good at following instructions. The desire to be godlike and master of all leads us to brilliance, to incredible technological advances — and also to ruin.

Central to Indigenous spirituality is the belief that the Earth is Mother. Following from this is the belief that it is necessary to live lightly on the land. Indigenous culture is infused with a different awareness of the Earth. According to this worldview, the living world and the worlds we cannot see are all contained in large circles — life that transitions, time that bends, life that goes on through and around us in a vast mystery. It was the early scriptures of the Hebrew testaments that first invented linearity. Time that has a beginning — and an end. With linearity came the notion of progress.

It was that transition that set us up for our current predicament. As York University professor Peter Timmerman once wrote, when we moved from being nomadic hunters, gatherers, and herders, to agriculture, our worldview changed.

In the initial understanding of the world, we had an Ontology of Abundance. There was enough. We believed that there would always be enough. When we were nomadic we had to pick up and move, so we did not acquire possessions, but nor did we need to carry surplus food for the next season. We had sufficient.

It was when we started growing food that we discovered the ability to start saving, hoarding, and guarding. We invented scarcity. There could never be "enough." We invented the fear of running out. We moved to an Ontology of Scarcity. And just as the Ontology of Abundance had given abundantly, the Ontology of Scarcity created scarcity.

In November 2013, my friend Patrick Lane, a brilliant poet, gone from us too soon, gave a remarkable speech in accepting his honorary degree from the University of Victoria. He told a story that sounded like a simple memory of his childhood. He described accompanying a group of hunters who, with the aid of a pack of dogs, had treed a cougar. "You watch as the man with the rifle climbs down from the saddle ... lifts the rifle, takes aim, and then ... and then you shrink inside a cowl of silence as the cougar falls. As you watch, the men raise their rifles and shoot them at the sun. You will not understand their triumph, their exultance. Not then.... You know now they shot at the sun because they wanted to bring a darkness into the world. Knowing that has changed you forever."

And so the poet told of how humanity has brought us to this place — a place of gathering darkness to the world.

And he told the story as one of appetites: "We began to eat the world. We devoured the oceans and we devoured the land. We drank the lakes and the seas and we ate the mountains and plains. We ate and ate until there was almost nothing left for you or for your children to come."

And this is why this book strikes the chord that asks us, "When is enough enough?"

We must care for the world. We must stop cannibalizing our own Mother. We must grow soil even more than food. We need science and Indigenous knowledge, and myth and faith.

We must tend our garden with love.

Elizabeth May *is the Leader of the Green Party of Canada and its first elected Member of Parliament, representing Saanich-Gulf Islands in southern Vancouver Island. She is an environmentalist, writer, activist, and lawyer.*

INTRODUCTION

MORE THAN ENOUGH

Is it not curious, that so vast a being as the whale should see the world through so small an eye, and hear the thunder through an ear which is smaller than a hare's? But if his eyes were broad as the lens of Herschel's great telescope; and his ears capacious as the porches of cathedrals; would that make him any longer of sight, or sharper of hearing? Not at all. — Why then do you try to "enlarge" your mind? Subtilize it.

— Herman Melville, *Moby Dick*

Agriculture's goal is to provide surplus food. The provision of this surplus relieves those who don't work the land or raise animals — factory workers, service providers, artists, politicians, lawyers, scholars, and others — of the task of growing food, allowing them to use their time and energy to engage in all of the other activities that contribute to the building of societies. So, clearly, agriculture is vital for functioning of healthy societies. However, today there is a crisis involving agriculture's ability to provide surplus food. The problem is not that agriculture is currently unable to provide the surplus necessary for healthy societies; rather, the problem is that the agricultural practices commonly used today are resulting in widespread environmental destruction, making their continued use unsustainable. This approach to overproduction has costs — significant ones. Today's surpluses are swallowing natural capital and tomorrow's productive capacity.

Ironically, our proclivity to address our fear of scarcity by overproducing is putting us on the path toward scarcity. Only by being appreciative of what Earth provides and respectfully accessing just enough can we achieve balance and sustainability.

When I was a boy, growing up on our farm in Wellington County, Ontario, food was respected. Our family understood, in a very fundamental way, the effort required to grow crops and raise animals for food. A natural result of this was that waste was limited to unavoidable losses. We were connected to the plants and animals on the farm and this relationship fostered feelings of responsibility and caring.

I loved to follow my grandfather during his chores, which seemed more of a joyful ritual than work. Pigs grunted expectantly and squealed with gratitude or greed, or perhaps both, when Grampa called them to the trough. Chickens yielded their eggs with remarkable grace as he gently retrieved the eggs from the nests, a skill I soon learned. Of course, the chickens would find their inevitable destination in the soup pot. In the meantime, they lived well with home-grown feed, clean nest boxes, opportunities to roam near the barn, and safety at night.

My grandfather and I drove to the pasture beyond the train tracks on the small yellow tractor my uncles had somehow extracted from the farm budget. As far as I know, Grampa used it only for this purpose. His team of horses, Pete and Joe, reliably leaned into their harnesses for the real work. When Grampa called the cattle, they appeared from the edges of the pasture and sometimes the shelter of an adjacent strip of trees. As he fed them, he talked to them and noted the state of their health. Usually they followed to see us off as we drove away. It wasn't until I was nine or ten that I realized that on most farms, cattle were chased rather than called.

It was from Grampa that I learned the wisdom of agriculture and what's really important. He died when I was seven. The agricultural knowledge I've learned since then has been mostly details. Somehow, with very few words, he demonstrated respect for soil, air, water, plants, and animals, and how they connect in a web of relationships.

I don't recall waste on the farm although there were certainly transformations — the "circular economy" of modern discourse. Nutrients would go from kitchen food scraps to pig feed to manure to soil, to be captured again by plants in Grandma's garden or Grampa's fields. Today, as I reflect on Grampa's farm, I feel sad about the general diminished awareness of how food is produced. Attitudes have changed; and instead of sustainable, self-sufficient food production, there is now industrial agriculture, with one-way flows that lead to excess. Nutrients in fertilizer, from off-farm, support plant growth for export crops, which often results in food loss and waste and concomitant nutrient loss into water bodies. In our rush to produce ever greater amounts of food, we are using up too many resources; our extravagance is unsustainable and will result in our being unable to meet the real needs of today and tomorrow.

Indigenous Peoples teach us to reflect on and learn from the experience of seven past generations and to anticipate our impact on seven future generations. Today, humans extract immense amounts of oil and gas from the earth to satisfy the "needs" of modern civilization. The burning of all of these hydrocarbons has resulted in the release of a huge amount of greenhouse gases (GHGs) into the atmosphere, causing climate change. We have ignored the knowledge passed on to us by previous generations about how to live with modest environmental impact; as a result, we are jeopardizing the health of the environment, of the plants and animals that we share the planet with, and in so doing we are undermining the ability of the next seven generations to live satisfied and secure lives.

If we were to travel back seven generations, we would find ourselves in the 1840s, when there were only about one billion people on Earth. In this period, there was not yet any industrial-scale drilling for oil; wood, coal, kerosene, and a few other resources provided the fuel for lighting, heating, and the primitive combustion engines that existed at the time. Astoundingly, humans now burn over one hundred million barrels of oil per day (Tertzakian, 2018). That is one big blaze, and it has resulted in an increase in atmospheric carbon dioxide (CO_2) concentration to over four hundred parts per million (ppm) — CO_2 is one of the major GHGs that contribute to global warming. In preindustrial times, the carbon dioxide concentration was only 280 ppm. A significant portion of the fuels consumed are used to produce, transport, process, package, and prepare food. Pollution from excess nitrogen fertilizer use, derived from fossil-fuel energy, is one of the greatest risks to current ecological stability. The sooner we learn to throttle back, the better will be our chances in the twenty-first century. To sustain ourselves, we need a long, steady flame.

Moving seven generations ahead will land us in the 2190s, when cheap oil and coal will have receded into the mists of history. Our descendants will wonder why we wasted so much fuel on one brief blaze, the biggest in Earth's history. They will wonder why we put the health of Earth, our only home, in jeopardy by indulging in such an excess of dangerous consumption.

We have the technology to extract and refine oil and gas, and our capacity to do so is increasing — fracking, the injection of high-pressure water into the earth to cause the release of oil and gas, accessing previously unobtainable hydrocarbon reserves, is one such new technology. And of course oil companies want to sell as much oil as possible to avoid the loss of current investments in potentially stranded assets. However, extracting and burning more and more hydrocarbons is causing real environmental damage and, in fact, threatens to cause a global calamity. The Intergovernmental Panel on Climate Change (IPCC) warns that we have less than twelve years to cut GHGs by at least half. We must develop ecofriendly, sustainable energy systems that will allow us to leave carbon-dense products in the ground: new technologies that will enable us to replace fossil fuels, avoiding their poisonous byproducts that have such negative impacts on climate systems.

Replacing fossil fuels with wind, solar, and tidal energy will allow us reduce GHG emissions and, so, will slow climate change. However, what is needed is not just the development of ecofriendly alternatives to fossil fuels: we must also work toward decreasing our energy consumption. The proliferation of high-speed modes of transportation, luxurious and excessively large buildings, and the overproduction of food, all supported by the exploitation of fossil fuels, must end. We need renewable-energy technologies, but we also need a reconsideration of how much rich food, high-speed transportation, housing space, and other modern benefits we actually need.

If we appreciate what we have, we are more likely to know when we have enough. Lynne Twist (2003) presents a compelling argument for sufficiency: "When you let go of trying to get more of what you don't really need, it frees up oceans of energy to make a difference with what you have. When you make a difference with what you have, it expands."

I have been approached by several friends who have chosen to sell their cars. In each case, they acknowledged how frightened they were about the sacrifice of not having a car on demand. This fear was mostly an issue before they sold their cars. All of them told me that as time went on without car ownership, they began to appreciate how free they were from payments, maintenance, insurance, licensing, parking, et cetera. They shifted from a sense of sacrifice to one of satisfaction. Granted, they all lived in cities and not rural areas.

In January each year, many of us resolve to eat well for our health. After the feasting of the December holiday season, we tend to focus on what we will go without, and, thus, will sacrifice. The benefits of sacrifice should not to be understated, but neither should they be overemphasized. Sometimes sacrifice is just sensible.

A few weeks of eating more fruits and vegetables balanced with protein, vitamins, minerals, and calories and eating less food with fat, salt, and sugar can result in feeling healthier and better satisfied. To continue healthy habits, it may be helpful to consider what makes our bodies feel good most of the time.

Michael Pollan's book *In Defense of Food* has a simple motto of only seven words, "Eat food, not too much, mostly plants." When I first read this motto, I wondered what else he expected us to eat, other than food. Right on cue, the first part of the book distinguishes real food (found on the outside walls of supermarkets) from "quasi-food" (the packaged and processed products found in middle aisles).

There are numerous words and phrases associated with eating well: "fellowship," "enough for all," "preserving, not wasting," "nutrition," "wholeness," "health," "vigour," "freshness," "savouring," "local culture," "favourite recipes," and so on. Eating well can be enjoyable and satisfying.

Today, food has become entertainment, and as with other forms of entertainment, we have become accustomed to instant gratification. Planning for a local and healthy seasonal basket of sustenance, preserving local produce, and preparing nutritious meals are at odds with immediate satisfaction. So many rich processed foods provide temporary pleasure. It is on this basis that they appeal and are advertised.

Nevertheless, an increasing number of people are drawn to planning and preparing healthy diets, diets that not only include nutritious foods but also are characterized by moderation. The challenge, or perhaps the trick, is to better convey to people the benefits of this, one of which is the satisfaction of feeling energetic, permanently.

Pierre Dansereau, a well-known biologist and ecologist from Quebec, passed away in 2011, one month shy of his one hundredth birthday. He believed that it is necessary to have a happy frugality (*austérité joyeuse*). The term is jarring. A happy frugality? This is a step beyond satisfaction. I don't think that he was advocating poverty; rather, I think that he wanted us to live our lives in a manner that allows us to obtain an adequate living without doing irreparable harm to the environment. To do that individually and collectively is to have a reason to be happy.

In evolved societies, and this is something evidenced, to some degree, in the Canadian social contract, there is a striving to ensure that everyone has enough to not only survive but to prosper. In Nova Scotia, a couple recently provided a wonderful example of what those with extra can do to help others to have enough. Allen and Violet Large donated most of their unexpected $11.2 million lottery winnings to family and local charities. Allen said, "We didn't need this big of an amount," and Violet noted, "There's somebody worse off than I am." They were happily frugal with their modest home, older car, and network of friends and family.

Before Violet died of cancer a short time later, she affirmed she was satisfied with their decision and was thankful of the opportunity to share their fortune to help ensure that others had enough. With such an attitude of gratitude, we become able to recognize when we have enough. Then we can make appropriate sacrifices, be satisfied, and sustain our lives with happy frugality.

❖

George Monbiot ends his book *Heat* on a downbeat. He worries that the campaign against climate change will be resisted because "it is for austerity, not plenty, for constraint, not freedom, and thus against ourselves." A campaign to create sustainable food production by showing the necessity of choosing less to avoid losing more, and by promoting sharing, even though that will result in having less to go around, faces similar hurdles. Yet, paradoxical as it seems, such a course can lead to more choice and greater freedom, while improving our chances for survival. Our current path of polluting the air and water and degrading the soil, while impacting climatic variability, has been shown to be already limiting our options, diminishing our access to things that we now take for granted. Changing course now will allow for a far greater range of possibilities in the future.

Currently, in our zeal for economic growth, we humans hoard goods, while degrading and polluting the soil, water, and air needed for sustainable agriculture. By shifting focus and facing facts, however, we can dampen the fossil flameout. We can regroup in a quest to eat well, in sustainable communities.

In 1798 the dour Reverend Malthus warned that if our human population increased exponentially, food production would still only increase linearly and the race of "man" could not escape from this law. A century or so later, Fritz Haber appeared to provide humanity with the means to escape the dire fate predicted by Malthus. The use of manufactured nitrogen fertilizer enabled food production to grow to an extraordinary degree; crop yields reached previously unrealized heights. Coupled with cheap energy, this new fertilizer seemed a godsend. Food production and human population increased exponentially like rapidly climbing jets in an air show.

However, as energy supplies dwindle and as greenhouse gas emissions increase as a result of the overuse of fossil fuels and nitrogen fertilizer, we might do well to give Malthus a second reading. His warning was, after all, a warning. Were he alive today, he would surely affirm that science based on ecological realism will serve us more effectively than science based on human hubris and fantasies of unlimited growth.

It's time for those of us in agriculture to say "Enough, already." Agriculturalists should no longer silently accept the status quo, one characterized by ever-increasing consumption and waste. We have a moral duty to yell "Stop!" Such a declaration is necessary to help change our course. It is hard to imagine that we are so addicted that we'll actually choose to sacrifice Planet Earth and ourselves, so it's time to revise our worldview and reject the gospel of perpetual economic growth. It's time to reimagine how we agree to make a living as individuals and together on Earth.

Our addiction to excess food is fueled (literally) by corresponding addictions to oil, gas, and coal. Addictions seduce and eventually control addicts by the comforts offered. But the oceans, forests, rangelands, and atmosphere cannot absorb much more of the GHGs from our big blaze of dwindling energy supplies. We need to consume less. We need to burn much less. Our choice is to adjust to Earth's bio-chemical limits or to face the consequences.

Apart from those engaged in subsistence farming, agriculturists have always been concerned with the question, "How will we feed the world?" Throughout history, farmers have worked, despite droughts, natural disasters, pest infestations, and disease, to try to ensure that humans are able to avoid not just famines but want of food generally, doing so in spite of rapidly increasing populations. This struggle is agriculture's *raison d'être*. Agriculturalists are convinced they're on the side of the angels. Feeding the world is a project to be proud of.

However, the more that agriculturalists have succeeded in "feeding the world" the greater the distance has become between those who eat the food and the specialists who grow, produce, and process it. Food has become a commodity, controlled largely by giant corporations. Modern agriculture has become stuck in a perpetual chase to provide excess commodities for an expanding market of consumers, each of whom is tempted to consume more. Of course, this extra consumption also leads to more waste per consumer. Globalized commodities benefit a select few financially. As for eaters, there are more who suffer illnesses from overeating than those who suffer from not getting enough.

If we continue to allow the population to grow, per capita consumption to increase, waste to mushroom, energy use to balloon, and pollution to spiral ever upward, Malthus's predictions will certainly be realized — it will only be a matter of time. If we follow the course we're on, there will eventually be collapse; it will be impossible to meet the world's needs, let alone its demands. Inevitably, there will be fear and famine. However, if we take steps now to moderate consumption, to eat well, and to dampen the big blaze, we will be able to control energy use and pollution and reduce our consumption levels to a sustainable carrying capacity. Following the latter path will involve producing and consuming just what's needed, using local initiatives, and learning to eat well in sustainable communities. Such a society might appear scrawny in comparison to the one produced by our current indulgence. It will be one typified by a joyous frugality. In time, food may once again be more associated with nurturing and sharing than with entertainment.

It's time to mature, get together, and work with what we have. If we continue to compete to consume more of the less that remains, we will have failed as a species. The consequences will be dire. If, on the other hand, we properly appreciate our special heritage and opportunity on Earth, if we adopt the necessary gratitude for what we have, then we will be able to lead balanced lives, ones that help foster a sustainable and nurturing planet.

1

INDIGENOUS FOOD SYSTEMS AS MILLENNIAL MODELS

Doesn't this mean that speaking in English, thinking in English, somehow gives us permission to disrespect nature? By denying everyone else the right to be persons? Wouldn't things be different if nothing was an it?

— Robin Wall Kimmerer, *Braiding Sweetgrass*

The Indigenous Peoples of Turtle Island (known to most as the continent of North America), lived on and cared for this land prior to the arrival of settlers. They did not do so for mere decades or centuries, but for millennia. Canada, as a current political jurisdiction on Turtle Island, is a relatively recent entity. We would do well to consider how the Indigenous civilizations that have existed in North America balanced production and consumption over the long haul.

Fundamental to this balance is respect. Increasingly, I understand that if food security is to be realized, then food must be treated with respect. I continue to learn how to respect food by pausing to be thankful for the process of plants combining sunlight energy, nutrients, and water to produce food, and then relishing each bite, while being sure not to waste food. We can learn from Indigenous hunters, who thank their prey animals before killing them and then judiciously use every part of the sacrificed animal.

Respect is shown by acknowledging the connections between humans, plants and animals, and Earth. Recognizing linkages is crucial. A short while ago, I asked an Indigenous colleague to speak to my Organic Agriculture class about Indigenous food systems. She said, "It would be a pleasure to talk to your class about Indigenous food and medicine." Instinctively, I responded by saying, "No, no. I doubt there will be time to talk about medicine, too. The class is only fifty minutes long." She kindly told me, "If I talk about food then I must also talk about medicine. They go together. It doesn't matter if there are five minutes or fifty minutes." Another lesson for me, even before her excellent class presentation started.

Food serves many functions, and it is necessary to recognize and respect all of these. It is also necessary to respect the land that provides us with food. Several years ago, Paul Wartman did his graduate research on forest garden systems (FGSs), multistoried plant communities providing food from vegetables, herbs, shrubs, and trees. The modern version of agriculture is focused on the economically efficient production of food commodities, using large-scale production of monocrops and large animal facilities. However, the attendant disrespect and waste result in ecological and social losses. To redress this emphasis, Paul wanted to explore more traditional food provisioning approaches. With energy, curiosity, and bits of advice from me and a colleague, he embarked on new research; and with grit he published two academic papers about FGS. It didn't take long for him to realize that the systems he was imagining had been practised over millennia by First Nations in Ontario. In his paper, "Temperate Agroforestry: How Forest Garden Systems Combined with People-Based Ethics Can Transform Food Systems," Wartman writes:

> In temperate regions of Turtle Island ... some areas such as Southern Ontario have largely been transformed from forest, wetland, and grassland to urban development and mono-culture agriculture.... [However, there is now a] shift away from monoculture agricultural practices and [with that a] resurgence of land-based, Indigenous systems is occurring. Forest garden systems (FGSs) present an opportunity to grow [food] for human needs using prac-tices that are environmentally regenerative, re-gionally appropriate to the ecology, and resil-ient to pests, diseases, drought, and economic changes.... In respectful collaboration, settler and Indigenous science systems can support the growth of skills to work with perennial plants and to share the principles necessary to create food systems centered upon a cul-ture that cares about people and recognizes its inextricable connection to the land and the water.... Southern Ontario's landscape, which

is traditional territory and home to over 133 First Nations and Metis communities, is made up of the mixed-wood plains ecozone in the north and is the Carolinian ecozone in the south, which is the most tree species-diverse zone in Canada, with more than 1600 plant species. These lands are traditional territory to the many First Nation communities of the Anishinabek, Haudenosauneega, Odawa, and Huron-Wendat Nations.... Prior to European contact, colonization, and settlement in the 18th and 19th centuries, S[outhern] Ontario had over 80% forest cover.... Compared to the minimal disturbance pre-colonization, there is now only approximately 10% forest cover remaining in S[outhern] Ontario. Development of settler agriculture and urbanization removed perennial vegetation from 70% of an entire landscape in under three hundred years.

In late 2018, I attended the Parliament of World Religions conference in Toronto, the first time this gathering had convened in Canada. It was an eclectic assembly, with people of many religions, of course, and from many parts of the world. Many of the attendees may have differed outwardly — there were people of different ethnicities among the group and various types of religious garments were on display — but there was, still, a sense of community, and all present shared expressions of concern and gratitude. It was clear that climate change, species loss, inequality, and intolerance required more heartfelt and thoughtful religious contributions. However, there was reciprocity in appreciating so many varied spiritual traditions.

I followed the Indigenous track for the weekend. In a time of rapid reporting of shallow scuttlebutt on social media, it was revealing to listen to First Nations' elders discuss the wisdom that is their inheritance from the many generations who have lived on this land. The elders introduced themselves with their spiritual names, as part of a clan and a nation, with a location. They held knowledge of who they are, and were, in a specific community, on a specific part of Turtle Island.

An elder who lives near the oil sands referred to the oil extraction on his ancestral land as the most concentrated example of bad medicine in all of North America. He spoke, too, of the caribou herds that his people have shared the land with and reminisced about the huge migrations that once took place. He spoke of how his people had lived respectfully with the caribou and lamented how different things are today, with the settler population controlling the land and making the decisions about its use. "The Porcupine caribou herd is the last healthy herd on Earth," he told us, "and the U.S. government is now planning to drill for oil in their calving grounds in Alaska. The four-leggeds cannot be abused like that."

The elder went on to say his people do not have a word for climate change. They refer to it as "unusual happenings." For example, animals formerly unknown to his people are moving north. "This year," he shared with the audience, "with a big clatter behind a friend's house, a racoon showed up. It does not have a Dene name. It had never been there. New plants are showing up, too, and suffocating some indigenous plants of the region."

An elder who lives in a community in the North, a community without clean water, expressed surprise that those of us who live in the south use litres of fresh water to flush the toilet every time we pee. She wondered how it was that we never run out of fresh water while so many communities up north have very limited amounts of water, their lakes and rivers having been contaminated by the tailings ponds of mines. "Why does industry have to be the boss of the land?" she wondered. Her comments made me question if my pension plan might be padded by the profits of companies not paying the complete costs for handling mining waste or oil sands effluents. In addition, I must ask myself, *Does the price of the stuff I am buying reflect the proper cost of its extraction and landscape disturbance?*

A younger woman, and yet also a grandmother, proclaimed, "I am an employee of Mother Earth. Our ancestors knew we were coming and didn't take too much, so we could live too. It is time to wake up." The necessity of a wake-up call was something repeated by many of the Indigenous speakers.

A spiritual teacher and respected elder succinctly contextualized the last millennium. "The Haudenosaunee Confederacy was a great civilization with a sophisticated political system of chiefs and clan mothers. Colonization changed that." Carrying pain from the past, she nevertheless pressed on to big questions of the present: "Will life continue on Earth or not? What am I doing to heal Mother Earth?" In a plea from the future, she declared, "Our great, great, great, great grandchildren want us to step up now."

❖

So much of Canadian territory extends into wilderness beyond a few hundred kilometres past the American border. Food systems in the North involve traditions of harvesting, with respect, the plants and animals native to the area. Most of us do not live in the remote regions of Canada and those who do are predominantly Indigenous Peoples, who have an ancestral stake in the land. To maintain spiritual, physical, emotional, and intellectual threads in a web of relationships, with respect for seven generations in the past and anticipating the needs of seven generations in the future, is to maintain relationships. A comprehensive and high "relational quotient" (RQ) includes relating to land, and the creatures and abiotic components of land.

Frequently, when discussions about living conditions in remote communities catch our awareness in the South, many wonder why we have to shell out more money to support the Indigenous people in those communities. "Why don't they just move?" is a question often asked. Would you move from a home that contains all of your spiritual, physical, emotional, and intellectual connections?

Stan Rowe, in his book *Home Place*, defines *ecosystem* as "a home system, a physical place surrounding us, to which we belong.… Not only are we in the Earth-envelope, we are parts of it, participants in it, born from it, sustained and reproduced by it."

Of course, we derive our modern lifestyle from Earth, too. As we enjoy a "luxurious living," it is tempting to see this "living," rather than Earth, as our cocoon and sustenance. We fail to appreciate the ultimate source of the benefits we enjoy. Like all other creatures of Earth, we have a right to live from Earth. However, it is vital that we also act to let Earth live. Neglecting Earth, because we are too busy being comfortable to notice, is not an option. Mother Earth will discipline us harshly, if necessary.

At the end of *Home Place*, Rowe writes: "[W]e have moments of enlightenment. Collectively and recurrently we show our truer colours, banding together to accomplish worthy goals, freely giving in the interests of a perceived higher good, responding to prophetic visions in times of crisis.... What Home Places need from us are more modest furnishings, less extravagance, more tender loving care."

Canada's sparsely populated land, its remote regions, is our land, too. Although such places lie far away from where most Canadians live, they nevertheless sustain us. They are not just reservoirs of resources. As the interconnectedness of ecosystems becomes more apparent, individuals are increasingly adopting more sustainable lifestyles; our society, too, is realizing, and responding belatedly, to its collective responsibilities. We might do well to accept more modest furnishings and less extravagance in populated areas, while supporting less populated areas.

Indigenous people and others who truly live on the land — those who see, hear, smell, taste, and move on Canada's expansive wilderness — embody a knowing worthy of attention. With familiarity of specific home places comes particular wisdom. Prudent decisions about land use, to help sustain a healthy Earth-envelope, require perceptive depth.

Food provisioning on land that is home is fundamentally about relationships.

> From the viewpoint of a private property economy, the "gift" is deemed to be "free" because we obtain it free of charge, at no cost.

> But in the gift economy, gifts are not free. The
> essence of the gift is that it creates a set of re-
> lationships. The currency of a gift economy is,
> at its root, reciprocity. In Western thinking,
> private land is understood to be a "bundle of
> rights," whereas in a gift economy, property
> has a "bundle of responsibilities" attached.
> (Kimmerer, 2013)

Clearly, these two ways of thinking are fundamentally at odds. Given this difference, one is forced to wonder if it will ever be possible to move forward together. Sarah Rotz, another graduate student I had the good fortune to advise, interviewed numerous farmers in southern Ontario. Their responses form the basis of a revealing paper she published, which derived its title from a statement made by one of the farmers she interviewed: "They took our beads, it was a fair trade, get over it. At the time they thought they were getting a real treasure. That is business, get over it" (Rotz, 2017).

Tension persists between a traditional Turtle Island gift economy (bundle of responsibilities) and a European legal framework of private property (bundle of rights). If we are to use our land well and eat well, i.e., if we are to adopt sustainable practices that will ensure that we will have food security for more than just decades (or even centuries), then the onus is on all of us to understand our responsibilities.

In 2011 the Tatamagouche Centre in Nova Scotia hosted a workshop, "Equipping Ambassadors of Reconciliation," in response to the injustices experienced by so many Indigenous people in residential schools. I attended because I had been moved by the exhibition "Where Are the Children: Healing the Legacy of the Residential Schools," presented earlier that spring at the Glooscap Heritage Centre, in Truro, Nova Scotia.

If I learned anything at the Tatamagouche workshop, it was that there is now an opportunity for all Canadians to develop a richer and more effective democracy. By addressing the roots of our collective narrow-mindedness and small-heartedness, we can join a widening circle of Canadians who want to transform our relationships and governance possibilities. Building relationships is not only essential for peace and understanding among people, it is also crucial for the future survival of humans and the animals and plants that we share the planet with. Sustainable relationships provide security. The lessons that we can learn from our Indigenous neighbours offer a collective growth opportunity for our hearts and souls.

Please listen and pay close attention when you read about or hear stories of residential schools. In a rich gesture of grace at the Tatamagouche workshop, one of the Indigenous elders who was abused at the Shubenacadie residential school invited us to walk beside her and other First Nations people. "That's all we ask," she said. "We don't want you to walk behind us or ahead of us. Just walk beside us and we'll learn and grow together."

To regain right relations as a society with the land that sustains all of us, it will be increasingly important to walk side by side with those who have recovering cultural perceptions about how to live sustainably. Indigenous knowledge systems may be more pertinent to sustaining food production capacity today than ever before.

The land and the sea of Canada give us life. The animals, plants, fertile soil, fresh water, and air sustain us. In 1604

Europeans were invited to join a respectful circle of people who knew how to live on this continent. Remarkably, after so much hurtful history, the invitation is still open.

Accepting the invitation in humility will help all of us to live fully in this country. Not only can we learn to live meaningfully with other people today, we can learn to live in the context of those who preceded us and those who will live many generations beyond us. Appreciation of our mixed blood and interdependence may soften our notions of "us" and extend our sense of family. Learning to live in harmony with, rather than by exploiting, our fellow creatures and the earth's non-living entities will deepen our potential for resilience. Be thankful for all our relations.

2

APPARENT CHOICE AND DECLINING FREEDOM

Our relatively benign climate of the past century is shifting, changing to a pattern of wobbly weather, one typified by less predictable trends. The source of this change, scientists agree, is the unusual increase in greenhouse gas emissions that has occurred over the period. Because of the changes in climate, agriculturalists, indeed, all of us, need to shift our world views accordingly.

Our system of food production is dominated by a few large-scale farm equipment manufacturers; fertilizer, seed, and pesticide suppliers; and food processors, distributors, and retailers. The market domination of these enterprises allows the corporations to control the market, achieve efficiencies of scale, and, so, maximize returns to investors. The wealth these players are able to squeeze from the system leaves little for those who actually grow the food and raise the animals that we eat. Farmers are left in the unenviable position of having to buy inputs (e.g., seed, fertilizers) at retail prices while being forced to sell their farm products at wholesale prices. In order to make a living, farmers have to do everything possible to lower per-unit costs for the produce they sell. So, is it any wonder that most farmers end up deciding to go with the flow and produce monocrop food products on a large scale?

And then there is the issue of debt. Most farmers, in order to purchase expensive machinery and to buy the necessary supplies at the beginning of each growing season, are forced to take on debt. Banks and the large corporations the farmers deal with extend credit to them to allow them to run their operations. The banks and corporations don't do this for free, of course; they charge interest, money that diminishes further the slim profits that farmers receive for their efforts.

Large-scale farm equipment manufacturers, fertilizer, seed, and pesticide suppliers, and lending institutions profit from the farmers. Food processors, distributors, and retailers are adept at securing profits from consumers. By encouraging the consumption of more and more processed and packaged foods, which cost more and produce greater profits than do simple, unprocessed foods, these companies have succeeded in creating a system that enables them to extract huge amounts of money from the compliant customers that they sell to.

If consumers grew more of their own food, prepared most meals from raw ingredients, and preserved the bounty at the end of each growing season, whether their own produce or that which is available at moderate cost, they would have more independence. Eating sustainably requires a rejection of the designed commodities of specialists. It requires making a real connection with the food we eat, and by extension with the environment that offers it and those who work the land to produce it.

Ideally, consumers would be involved in the cultivating of the food that they also eat. Such food provisioning can be done by individuals (or couples or families) acting alone; it can also be something that involves the larger community. This activity is collaborative, involving time and skills, and is based on an appreciation of the value of healthy food and an understanding of the importance of ensuring the long-term capacity of our ecosystem to provide it. To the extent that engaged consumers observe and touch soil, plants, animals, and the foods that are derived from these, they will be more food self-reliant.

Most people don't consider the issues of power and freedom when they think of food production and consumption, but, in fact, these issues are fundamental. For example, when the Soviet Union still existed, people in the West tended to feel some smugness about the failure of the Soviet food system. There was too much central control, it was claimed, and this left very little initiative for those who cared for the soil and tended crops and animals. Surpluses were meagre. A lack of freedom resulted in failure. Dostoyevsky's *The Brothers Karamazov*, and, in particular, his poem the "Grand Inquisitor," which is contained within the novel, both haunt and inspire me. For years I've seen them as a parable of the concentration of power in our food system.

The story is set in sixteenth-century Spain, during the Inquisition. In the tale, Christ returns to Earth for a visit and arrives in Seville. He wants to quietly visit his children during their suffering. While in Seville, he is inspired to perform a few miracles to heal some of his distraught followers; these actions attract the attention of the Grand Inquisitor. This aged cardinal of the Cathedral of Seville promptly jails Christ and then privately questions him. The Grand Inquisitor wants to know why Jesus, his prisoner, is daring to meddle, especially given that it had taken the Church fifteen hundred years to tidy up the mess left by Christ's last visit.

The Grand Inquisitor talks while his prisoner listens. "Was it not you who said so often in those days, 'I shall make you free'?" After chastising the prisoner for offering more freedom than men (gender-neutral language was not a strength of the Grand Inquisitor) could bear, the Grand Inquisitor goes on to argue that the Church had vanquished freedom to make men happy. He asserts that Christ, when tempted in the wilderness, should have turned the stones into bread.

> But you did not want to deprive man of freedom and rejected the offer, for, you thought, what sort of freedom is it if obedience is bought with loaves of bread? You replied that man does not live by bread alone.… [W]e [the Church leaders] alone shall feed them in your name, and we shall lie to them that it is in your name. Oh, without us they will never, never feed themselves. No science will give them bread so long as they remain free.

The Grand Inquisitor continues to scold, or, perhaps, as Ivan, the storyteller, hints, to confide in the prisoner. At the end of his long life, the Grand Inquisitor feels the burden of carrying the freedom of the followers of Christ who have surrendered theirs to the Church in exchange for being fed. He believes they realize there cannot be enough freedom and bread for everyone, that they will never be able to let everyone have their fair share.

> There are three forces, the only three forces that are able to conquer and hold captive forever the conscience of these weak rebels for their own happiness — these forces are: miracle, mystery, and authority.... [F]or what man seeks is not so much God as miracles.... [W]e too were entitled to preach a mystery and to teach them that it is neither the free verdict of their hearts nor love that matters, but the mystery which they must obey blindly, even against their conscience. So we have done. We have corrected your great work and have based it on miracle, mystery, and authority.

The Grand Inquisitor carries on with his disturbing story and the conviction that people want to be fed, more than anything else.

> In receiving loaves from us, they will, of course, see clearly that we are taking the loaves made by their own hands in order to distribute them among themselves, without any

miracle. They will see that we have not made stones into loaves, but they will in truth be more pleased with receiving them from our hands than with the bread itself! For they will remember only too well that before, without us, the bread they made turned to stones in their hands, but that when they came back to us, the very stones turned to bread in their hands. They will appreciate only too well what it means to submit themselves to us forever!

Today the spectacular cathedrals of commerce draw our eyes and imaginations up toward fantastic possibilities. Isn't it interesting that the large food corporations, just like farmers, use slogans such as "feeding the world" to put a positive spin on their operations? I wonder if some CEOs would argue that "they (the people) will never, never feed themselves."

The Grand Inquisitor would probably not be surprised by the general compliance and lack of questioning displayed by many of those fed. The miracles of food technology, employed in the huge plants that process the food that provides comfort and happiness, tend to dazzle.

There is mystery in the food chain; for the average consumer, the workings of the whole system are impossible to understand. There are so many elements: the huge fields of monocrops and confined animal feeding operations and storage facilities; the complex transport systems; the food processing plants; the source-obscuring labels; and the retail outlets. There is the authority of corporations and governments, too. Their rules of food safety seem designed so that only large companies can meet them; increasingly, small producers, processors, distributors, and marketers are marginalized.

Why do so many continue to accept "bread," i.e., the packages of processed food that offer convenience and tastes (sweet, salty) designed to satisfy our most primitive cravings, from the hands of those who exploit farmers, manipulating and impoverishing those who struggle to maintain soil health and protect their ecosystems?

Today, the food system delivers excess to feed our greed. In the course of doing so, 40 percent of the food produced in North America is wasted; that is how the current system works. There is a risk of assuming this system is normal and perpetual. There is a risk we will continue to give up freedoms and food self-reliance to those who now control the food production system, allowing them to manage the system, allowing them to reap huge profits, helping to sustain a deeply flawed system to function, until it cannot.

3

PUSHING PRODUCTION TO ADDRESS POPULATION GROWTH

He who binds to himself a joy
Does the winged life destroy
But he who kisses the joy as it flies
Lives in eternity's sun rise

— William Blake, "Eternity"

When my daughter was a toddler, we constructed a unique snowman. Odd bulges distinguished our creation from other snow creatures, and she giggled at her new buddy. I was distressed, the next morning, to realize that older children in the neighbourhood had smashed our creation. How could I explain this to a three-year-old who had put all her heart into this project? I chose my words carefully and with some gravity explained what had happened. Her refreshing reaction helped me gain perspective. "That's OK. Now we can do it again and build another one."

In December 2013, I read an article by George Monbiot in the *Guardian* that summarized research reported in the journal *Motivation and Emotion*. "As people become more materialistic, their wellbeing diminishes. As they become less materialistic, it rises." He goes on to describe children in a church program gaining self-esteem as they practised more sharing and saving, avoiding spending. Then he talks about the loneliness of a man with four Rolex watches, "one Rolex short of contentment," because that man knew of another man who had five.

If we truly wish to sustain human civilization, we need to make an honest assessment of what we want to keep and what changes need to be made to ensure that we are able to do so. Once, at a farm meeting, some speakers expressed exasperation with their situation, claiming that it was nearly impossible to make a living from farming. "It partly depends what you mean by *a living*," was the sole comment of an older farmer in the corner.

Sustaining ourselves, and Earth, involves more than improving efficiencies. A reassessment of what we really need is necessary, too; with that we can devise a sustainability strategy. Knowing what is not needed, or what is too much, is a necessary part of the calculation. The status quo may not represent our real needs; in fact, it can distract us from discerning what our real needs are.

Since the emergence of life on Earth, the increasing complexity of life forms and of the interconnectedness between them has been stunning. We are blessed as humans to have developed science and technology to help us appreciate the wonder of our biosphere and how it functions.

Science and technology have also allowed humans to greatly improve their quality of life — the achievements made in health care provide an example of how human knowledge can help to make our lives better. Some developments have very negative effects, however — some obvious, some not so obvious. Until the twenty-first century, Westerners have tended to see our ever-increasing ability to extract resources from the earth and to harvest the plants and animals found on it as a good thing. This has led not just to an ability to satisfy basic needs; it has also led to a tendency to luxuriate in excess. To narrow our creative abilities by pursuing more material wealth is to shortchange our future. Even if this was a primary human requirement under past conditions, it is time to see where we are now and to pivot to the next challenge of survival.

Political and business success in our society is tied to maintaining and, where possible, increasing the rate of economic growth, usually to advance materialism. Today, we face new challenges: finding better ways to generate energy from renewable and non-polluting sources; reviving biodiversity; maintaining clean air and water, and healthy soil, as well as other resources; and adapting to a changing climate, even as we mitigate human activities that exacerbate the buildup of greenhouse gases in the atmosphere.

A further challenge is to distribute income and resources fairly to sustain societal stability. People who resist this idea usually fall back on a couple of well-worn arguments to support their position. Let's examine those.

Opponents of income redistribution argue that people who work hard and take risks (that is to say, the rich) deserve more. The reality is, most impoverished people work extremely hard, too, and every day they risk (voluntarily or not) almost everything they have, which may be small in comparison to the resources of the wealthy but is, in proportion to their income and assets, enormous. Of course, despite their efforts, they do not get what the rich do. So, reward is mostly unrelated to effort or to risk. Many rich people are no more deserving of their wealth than the poor are of their poverty.

Those who favour the status quo will sometimes acknowledge the inequity of things as they currently exist, but claim that there is no need to take any direct action to correct the situation — the problem will, they say, be addressed by simply increasing productive capacity. The claim is wearing thin. Time and again, so-called trickle-down economics has been shown to be of no help in improving the lives of the poor.

Given all of this, there is no question that reassigning productive capacity, in an equitable system, merits exploration.

By remaining unduly attached to the growth of materialism, we are not only endangering our survival and the survival of life on Earth, we are also missing the potential of a new quality of life in which we could thrive. Part of that potential involves "kissing the joy as it flies." Material possessions can serve us adequately. Do we also want to emotionally invest in them, such that they capture our joy?

The joy we cling to, as a society, is economic growth. But does it, in fact, bring us joy? The attachment to economic growth and the acquisition of material wealth has produced the dominance, violence, and authoritarianism that have characterized most human societies in the last seven thousand years. Many assume that this pattern is the only one possible, that human nature will always result in such a world. However, if we examine human history more closely and travel farther back in time, we will see that alternative ways of being can exist, and, indeed, have existed. In fact, Riane Eisler in *The Chalice and the Blade* draws our attention to a long period of dynamic equilibrium and partnership in the past, a period that lasted for possibly as long as thirty thousand years — more than four times the seven thousand years of the current dominator patterns. What if we were to re-create ourselves and our relationships and our culture in the partnership models revealed by Eisler? Maybe we could reprogram our societies so that they are built on the foundation of both social and ecological justice, while drawing from deeper roots. The emphasis on community and pacifism within Mennonite communities, the pattern of partnership that I experienced on my grandfather's farm, may offer a model to help us return to deeper roots.

It is common to hear that achieving better efficiencies, by intensifying our use of the resources that we extract from nature will help us reduce the burden on Mother Earth. Let's take a look at this claim.

It's possible to increase the overall fuel efficiency of automobiles by encouraging more people to drive smaller cars — multiplying the number of drivers who own vehicles that use only six litres of gas for each one hundred kilometres, rather than, for example, pickup trucks, that use twelve litres for the same distance.

We know that fossil fuel use and greenhouse gas emissions should be reduced. However, we won't get there by only intensifying the use of fuel per vehicle. It helps, but it's not enough. It is also necessary to reduce the number of car trips taken while also increasing the number of people in each vehicle. Doing such things is good, too, but, again, it's not enough. It's vital that we take in the big picture: keeping our eyes on total oil use and total GHG emissions offers a better way of effectively monitoring increases and decreases of overall harm.

Despite various efforts to improve fuel efficiency, we are now burning one hundred million barrels of oil per day across the globe. About a decade ago, it was eighty-five million barrels of oil per day. Global oil consumption is still rising despite intensification efforts.

GHG emissions in Canada peaked in 2007 at 734 megatonnes (Mt) of carbon dioxide equivalent (CO_2eq) and rapidly declined to 682 Mt CO_2eq in 2009, a figure not seen since 1996. Recessions can have benefits. Since 2012, Canada has produced more than 700 Mt CO_2eq every year. GHG emissions are stubbornly persistent in our fair land.

❖

Many farms optimize food commodity output per dollar input (cost efficiency) by finding ways to produce as many kilograms of food as possible. For example, the purchase of a large tractor and equipment to seed and harvest corn and soybean fields can be deemed a cost-efficient move if more kilograms of corn and soybean are produced than could be done with the older equipment. This cost efficiency can be further enhanced if it's possible to use only one operator to cover many hectares in one day.

The 2012 Field to Market report trumpets the steady decline, over three decades, in the amount of resources required to grow one bushel (bu) of corn in the United States. These resources include land, soil (less lost as a result of erosion), water for irrigation, and energy. This decline in resources used per bushel produced has been accompanied by a reduction in the release of greenhouse gases.

That sounds good; however, there's a question that needs to be answered: What impact did the use of these resources have on the environment? It turns out that the average resource requirement per bu was about 40 percent less. The even better news was that soil erosion decreased by 60 percent per bu of corn.

In this period, average U.S. corn yields increased from about 100 bu per acre to 150 bu per acre, a 50 percent increase, given continual crop genetic and management improvements. U.S. corn production increased from 6.6 billion bu to 9.5 billion bu in the same thirty-year span. These average yields are now north of 170 bu per acre and total production was at 14.6 billion bushels in 2017. This concentration of one crop over so many acres invites diseases and weeds to adapt and prosper. The response — increasing levels of crop protection pesticides — compounds environmental stress.

Thus, even though resource use per bu went down, the environment was actually impacted more severely, with more bu. The net effect of the increase in the amount of corn produced was the use of more land, more irrigation water, and more energy. This increased use of resources resulted in more greenhouse gas emissions.

Sustainable intensification is usually advocated by those who believe that if there are more people and there is more prosperity there will of course be more consumption and thus more production. "Sustainable intensification looks at whole landscapes, territories, and ecosystems to optimize resource utilization and management. Farmers must produce more from the same area of land and use fewer inputs while producing greater yields. Such a transition is both possible and necessary" (FAO, n.d.).

Is this transition really possible? Is it really necessary? If the patterns of yields per acre, total production, and resource use continue, then the transition will still lead to more negative overall environmental impacts. If we continue to consume as much per person as we do now, and if we continue to waste over one-third of available global food, then, yes, it will be necessary. However, it is not axiomatic that we *must* forge ahead with careless consumption.

We can eat less; we should eat less. Two-thirds of healthcare costs in Canada can now be attributed to chronic diseases associated with unhealthy eating (Dubé et al., 2009). The overconsumption of food causes more illness than does lack of food. We can reduce the wastage of food; we must do so. At present, Canadians waste approximately 40 percent of all available food in the country. This is unconscionable. There are benefits to be had with sustainable intensification, but as we learn to grow more with less, we also need to rise to the challenge of consuming and wasting less food. Doing so will allow us to reduce the need to produce as much food as we do today.

Gambling that sustainable intensification alone will maintain Earth's ecological health will fail. I am an aggie and respect what those who have been working to advance sustainable intensification have achieved. Nevertheless, if we are to feed ourselves and at the same time maintain the health of the planet, it is necessary to explore other approaches, too. It will be a slow and steady process. Rushing and competing to produce an excess of food, food that will inevitably be sold at a cheap price, leads to waste and loss of production capacity. Soil on farmland has been steadily degrading, while our reliance on production with fossil-fuel energy has risen and water extraction for irrigation has increased. We live in a world of too much food: the solution to our problem is not to pathologically keep producing beyond what we need.

Wendell Berry, the author of *Life Is a Miracle* and many other essays and books about farming, first elucidated the idea that there is value in increasing the ratio of eyes per acre. The more eyes engaged in observing each unit of land, he argues, the better the opportunity to know the land and coax sustainable yields from it, to benefit without doing harm. Unfortunately, the trend is running in the opposite direction; today, there are fewer and fewer eyes on the land. Farms are increasing in size and more machinery is being used to do the work formerly done by hand — all of this is happening in the rush to improve "efficiency" in order to obtain higher yields per day of each person's labour. As a result, there is less observation of the land, and less reflection concerning what the observed changes might mean and what the appropriate responses to the small signals from all of the particular sites on the land might be.

When many hectares of farmland are aggregated, and the understanding of the land is transformed into information averaged in statistics, we lose the particular knowledge of the land that was held by my grandfather and that has been held by farmers throughout history. In spring, my grandfather stood on the running board of his horse-drawn seed drill, set to apply the minimum rate of seed to the whole field, and was fully aware of the soil sliding beneath him. In more fertile areas of the field, which he knew by head and heart, he scooped his hand into the grain of the drill box to toss arcs of seed, thus increasing the seeding rate where it would return dividends. Modern GPS devices can only partially compensate for the lack of his type of awareness, because they are designed to answer very specific questions — they can only do what they've been designed to do — and do not translate the nuanced messages understood by a person who has experience on the land observing, listening, smelling, feeling, and sometimes tasting.

Agricultural ecosystems are made up of delicately connected webs that link the sun, plants, animals, people, soil, water, and air, and the energy and nutrients that flow among them. When components of the ecosystem are harmed or the flows of energy and nutrients are restricted, the cost to the regenerative capacity of the agricultural ecosystem goes up.

Grampa may not have maximized food output on his farm per dollar input, per unit of land, or per person; however, the regenerative capacity of his farm was evident. When the team of horses worked well together, time and stress were saved and we felt the assurance of on-farm possibilities. The manure he hauled to the field maintained soil fertility. The horses, capable of reproducing themselves and maintaining themselves with hay and oats from less than 25 percent of the farm area, contributed to the regenerative capacity of the farm. It was set to hum for years to come.

In later years, in order to facilitate much higher crop output, the farm required higher inputs of fossil fuel embedded in manufactured nitrogen fertilizer, herbicides, and tractor power to produce corn year after year on soil that eroded, became more compacted, lost soil organic matter (SOM), and depended on external inputs. Grampa's well-balanced series of relationships on the farm was put under strain and the regenerative capacity of the farm was much lower.

Modern efficiencies, many traced to agriculture, have spurred growth. It must be understood that organisms do not consciously manipulate their reproduction and population growth; rather, they respond to their environmental resources in apparently predictable trends. They appear to follow a strategy of population growth.

Ecological theory describes r-strategists and k-strategists. R-strategists colonize new niches rapidly and their population grows exponentially, i.e., the time to double their population is half as long with each new doubling. When the population of r-strategists becomes too great for available resources to sustain it, it crashes. I think of r-strategists as raiders, and they continue to raid resources until their consumption exceeds sustainable levels.

In contrast, k-strategists maintain stability: their population increases to a sustainable level and then hovers around it. They adjust to the resource-carrying capacity of their environment and, therefore, more of them survive longer. I call k-strategists keepers. They keep population, consumption, and waste at levels to maintain their population in balance with required resources.

Are humans raiders or keepers? The human population did not reach one billion until 1830. Then it doubled relatively quickly — within one hundred years. The next doubling, to four billion, occurred in 1975, only forty-five years later. Had the exponential growth trend continued, our population would have broken through eight billion in 1997. However, our population, more than twenty years beyond 1997, is now just 7.6 billion, indicating a slowing growth rate. Although acknowledging that the United Nations Population Division has forecasted a world population above twelve billion by 2100, the International Institute for Applied Systems Analysis, alternatively, has predicted that it will increase to 9.2 billion by 2050, peak at 9.4 billion in 2070, and then ease down to nine billion by 2100 (Lutz et al., 2014).

As we trudge determinedly into the twenty-first century, I fear that, whatever level the world's population settles at, it is inevitable that, as more food is produced for more people, and as there is more consumption per person and more waste per person, the demands of humanity on the world's resources will exceed capacity and there will be a crash. Unless we become keepers quickly, the inevitable lean years will be leaner and meaner than most of humanity can cope with.

Agriculture has become the generator of surpluses that permit economic growth. We may not see ourselves as raiders, but in effect we are. With more growth, agriculture has not only met the market demand for food but has gone beyond and created even greater surpluses. The illusion of the inevitability of surpluses, however, is fooling fewer people as food prices rise and the world's most vulnerable are at increasing risk of hunger. Surpluses in recent decades swallowed both current capital and tomorrow's regenerative capacity. More surpluses permitted more freedom for people to engage in activities in our society that are not tied to food production. Thus, modern agriculturalists are proud of the fact that in 1900, one Canadian farmer could feed 10 people and today one feeds 120 people (Mathews, 2015). Not only have we achieved this widening ratio, but we've also continued to feed the growing population. What could be more honourable?

Despite our experience in the last two centuries, the human population does not have to increase. Material, energy, and food consumption per person could decline considerably. Waste per person can be eliminated, when all materials not required in a given process or product become the input material for other processes and products. Those who explore potential plant production in space at the Controlled Environment Systems Research Facility at the University of Guelph (ces1.ces.uoguelph.ca/index.shtml) are clear that space food systems cannot allow waste, but rather require cycling of nutrients, water, and gases. May this wisdom land on Earth.

It is possible for us to feel good about using our resources well and to stretch, excel, and actualize ourselves in the visual arts, drama, music, dance, literature, crafts, storytelling, meditation, spiritual rituals, and other distinctly human activities.

Douthwaite (1992) reminds us that for people in a country to be fed, clothed, housed, educated, and entertained to an excellent standard does not take a high level of consumption, unless it is extraordinarily wasteful.

I recall being surprised as an undergraduate student when I read Adam Smith, who asserted that Europeans should take land from the Indigenous Peoples because Europeans would derive more value from it than the Indigenous Peoples could. In the twenty-first century, we are still extracting as much monetary value as possible, per hectare of arable land, to fuel economic growth. The theory is that growth will trickle down to lift all economic boats of individuals and families.

Joseph Stiglitz, the former chief economist of the World Bank, in *Globalization and Its Discontents*, writes, "Despite repeated promises of poverty reduction made over the last decade of the twentieth century, the actual number [not percentage] of people living in poverty has actually increased by almost 100 million. This occurred at the same time that total world income actually increased by an average of 2.5 percent annually."

Have all the beliefs and actions and calls of raiders for economic growth come to this? More global income results in more poor people than ever?

Who is enjoying the accumulating wealth, if not the intended beneficiaries of development programs who were highlighted in the lectures of my well-meaning undergraduate professors? Mark Buchanan, in his 2002 essay "The Science of Inequality," discusses the "Pareto distribution":

> It ... implies that a small fraction of the wealthiest people always possess a lion's share

of a country's riches. It is quite easy to imagine a country where the bulk of people in the middle of the distribution would own most of the wealth. But that is never so. In the United States, about 80 per cent of the wealth is held by 20 per cent of the people, and the numbers are similar in Chile, Bolivia, Japan, South Africa and the nations of Western Europe. It may be 10 per cent owning 90 per cent, 5 per cent owning 85 per cent, or 3 per cent owning 96 per cent, but in all cases, wealth seems to migrate naturally into the hands of the few.

And it is getting worse. The global rich in the top 1 percent experienced a bump in their share of the total of worldwide wealth from 42.5 percent when the 2008 financial crisis peaked to just over 50 percent ($140 trillion) in 2017 (Neate, 2017). One is left wondering why so many of us accept the dogma of economic growth when so few of us benefit. Even if we work hard and make our economy sizzle, the wealth we generate will probably accrue to someone who already has too much.

Regardless of the economic efficiencies, discussed earlier in this chapter, that often come when farm ownership is concentrated in fewer hands, there are also disadvantages. For example, dependence on perpetual fossil-energy flows and the complex system of manufacturing, crop and livestock production, processing, distribution, and wholesale-retail marketing maintained by fossil energy is vulnerable to shocks of price and energy-supply disruption. In the 1990s, when my first-year students toured farms, they had ten questions to ask each farmer. One question was about the implications for the farm if energy prices doubled. One farmer explained that the cost of diesel fuel and electricity was small in proportion to other costs, such as feed, so he wasn't too worried about the prospect of higher energy prices. The thing is, the cost of feed, building materials, machinery, fertilizer, and pesticides will all rise if energy prices go up.

If energy prices rise significantly, no level of expert post-shock management will cope as well as numerous trained eyes, hands, and feet on small parcels of land, engaged by some aspect of ownership or long-term tenure. Skilled and committed farmers, keepers, if you will, have a chance to adapt to these shocks on familiar farms that are small enough to be hollered across.

Will poverty increase without economic growth? If income distribution does not accrue proportionally to the poorest during periods of growth, many fear that, without growth, the poorest will suffer even more (Saunders, 2008). It will be tough to give up the addiction to economic growth. Governments will struggle when population and economic growth plateau, and the increasing average age of citizens leaves fewer working adults to pay taxes. Ecological justice for Earth and other species will not be achieved without social justice, i.e., the fair distribution of resources and wealth among all classes, genders, and races of people. If the burden on our ecosystems must be relieved by stopping economic growth (and I think it must, despite all the implications of doing so), then we must use our human creativity and capacity for collaboration to manage resources as keepers in such a way that the poorest among us can survive. We're running out of the ecological license that has allowed us to dodge issues of social justice by growing the economy each year — a practice that provides just enough to prevent revolt by those who lack, while still accumulating more in the treasure chests of those who indulge.

Is it possible that our apparent servitude to the narrative that economic growth "raises all boats" is simply a bad habit? George Monbiot ("We Should Welcome a Recession," 2007) argues that "[g]rowth is a political sedative, snuffing out protest, permitting governments to avoid confrontation with the rich, preventing the construction of a just and sustainable society." If this is true, then why do we elect governments who hide behind the growth mantra? Why do those of us engaged in agriculture continue to grow more food, fuel, and fibre, more quickly, so that our population, consumption per person, and waste per person can expand?

Mike Nickerson, in *Life, Money and Illusion*, argues that advertising encourages us to consume more, and often more than we need, thus causing waste and needless environmental problems. Not only is that bad, but businesses are allowed to claim advertising as an expense to reduce their tax contributions. Nickerson recommends that businesses, including his, should advertise completely with their own dimes, without rebates from the public purse. It doesn't make sense that taxpayers should be forced to underwrite an activity that encourages excess consumption and waste. Nor does it make sense that the public should be stuck with the bill to clean up extraction sites for materials to produce the excess goods and then the waste that results from that overproduction. The financial costs are accumulating: they will be borne by our children and grandchildren. As well, those children and grandchildren, not to mention all the other species we share the planet with, will suffer the environmental damage we are causing now. Do we want them to continue paying for our excesses long after the bursts of quarterly profits have passed? Surely their genuine needs warrant at least the same priority as our current wants.

Society's excess consumption is not possible to sustain, so let's bring advertising to account. Why should our money be spent to reward the efforts of those who try to persuade us to buy more and more, whether or not we need more, or even want it.

Thomas Homer-Dixon in *The Upside of Down* explores our attachment to economic growth, and how we are denying imminent catastrophe by blindly extending our ride on the growth curve. Drawing on Buzz Holling's theory of the adaptive cycle, Homer-Dixon argues that by delaying collapse, our highly complex and globalized society, when it does inevitably crash, will experience immense devastation, with rippling implications that will be long-lasting and far-reaching. An alternative to sticking with the apparent benefits of growth at all costs is instead to elicit small collapses that stimulate the resilience response. Thus, creativity is released, and reorganization, in ways not evident prior to the collapse, becomes possible.

Redundancy, with its implications of overlap, is the capacity to do the same function in several ways while holding more in reserve than is normally required. Paul Hawken (2007) in *Blessed Unrest* reminds us of the benefits of loosely connected organizations and the fact that many such explore overlapping and yet slightly different approaches. He compares the apparently random and overlapping organization of numerous volunteer organizations to similar networks in natural ecosystems.

If one of the costs of redundancy is overlapping efforts and extra supplies in warehouses, then so be it. The biblical Joseph interpreted the Egyptian pharaoh's dreams about seven lean cows eating seven fat cows and advised the pharaoh to set aside one-fifth of the available grain during the predicted seven years of good crops to prepare for a following seven years of poor yields and famine. The pharaoh believed Joseph and hired him to oversee the storage of grain. The kingdom prospered during the seven years of famine, while neighbouring countries faced starvation. Survival requires serious investment. Homer-Dixon acknowledges the contribution of redundancy to resilience. A local region will improve its resilience with warehouses of local food supplies, something that should be done even when food can still be easily imported from anywhere with rolling stocks of just-in-time delivery. The incentive for such redundancy is to prepare for the collapse of the growth cycle when the flows of just-in-time delivery will dry up.

We act as if economic growth is inevitable and indefinite. This too will pass. Economic growth only proceeds because enough of us agree to participate in the current orgy of consumption and waste. The economist Kenneth E. Boulding grounded his audiences with the quote, "Anyone who believes exponential growth can go on forever in a finite world is either a madman or an economist."

What if they called for economic growth and nobody participated? What if everyone consumed and recycled as keepers and as if we intended to live here with all other species for many generations? Eventually, perhaps very soon, we will reach the top of the growth curve. It is the destiny of biological organisms. Nevertheless, with some partnership and planning we may learn to eat and live sensibly, and not crash like raiders inevitably will. We could cast our lot as keepers.

4

BALANCING PRODUCTION AND CONSUMPTION

Farmers produce more food than what is sold, and retailers and others sell more than what is consumed. More consumers suffer from eating too much food than those who suffer from eating too little (Hamzelou, 2012). By 2025, there will be 2.7 billion overweight and obese adults, one-third of the global population. Many of them will need medical care (Boseley, 2017).

Our goal should be to sustain sufficient production, enough only for adequate, healthy consumption. Of course, given the contingencies of volatile weather patterns, which are likely to get worse, the balance will never be exact and some redundancy of stored supplies will be necessary. However, production goals could be set to provide the healthy food that is needed, in appropriate amounts. The current *modus operandi* is to produce as much as the market demands and will bear and then more, just to be sure.

In 1966, the global population was only 3.4 billion, about 45 percent of today's count of 7.6 billion. Since then, almost every serious agricultural report or meeting starts with a nod to the requirement to increase food production in order to feed the nine billion–plus people expected to be here by 2050. The straightforward appeal of increasing tonnes of food each year is measurable and possible, even if a clear challenge. With imagination and hard work, we can produce more tonnes of food; food to nurture and support more lives each year.

For those working in agriculture, engaging in an activity whose purpose is to feed the world is a source of great pride. And the achievements of farmers should be celebrated. There is a problem, however, with the method by which those achievements have been obtained. To feed all of the world's people, it has come to be assumed that industrial-scale farming, i.e., hyperproductive, large-scale cultivation, is essential. This method involves a one-way supplier model: products flow in one direction, from farm suppliers to farms to processors to retailers and, finally, to receptive consumers. The process involves specialization at each step, and consumers have no input — they only consume.

There is a better way, an approach that would involve changing things so that we eat well in our sustainable communities. How can we design food systems of knowledgeable participants who willingly offer enough time and energy and money to eat delicious food that nourishes all of us adequately? If I were the minister of education, I would strive to introduce a food curriculum in all schools, running from Kindergarten to Grade 12. In addition to training food-aware citizens to eat well, this curriculum would give students the knowledge, as they learn about math, science, social studies, and geography, to understand the issues involved in food production and consumption; it would help them to learn how to eat well, how to eat in a way that is healthy for them, the economy, and the environment.

Patience and time will be required. Children know so little about food because the adults in their lives have relegated food to purchasable items, hardly distinguishable from crayons, games, and phones. Our long-term project should be to teach as many children as possible about food. We can aspire to teach them well, so that they will recognize opportunities for change when they are old enough to make decisions with impact in our parliaments, businesses, and homes. In the meantime, may we remember that the most effective way of teaching is to model what is professed.

When I was five, Mom wanted me to go with her to Kitchener to see the Queen of England. "What do we *do* when we see the Queen?" I asked. "We'll stand on the sidewalk and watch her go by in a big, black car with no roof and when she sees us, we'll wave. If we're lucky the car might stop and she might actually say, 'How do you do?'"

"Oh," I ventured with less enthusiasm than Mom expected for royalty.

"If the Queen's not good enough for you, you can help Grampa in the barn."

"Oh-h-h," I almost sang, being enough of a diplomat not to increase my voice pitch too much.

"Grampa's hauling manure today," she said smugly.

"Oh, OK, can I help?" My blurt was out and I waited worriedly for her backhand comment. Her silence finally dissolved in a disbelieving hiss of, "Get ready to go to the barn."

In the barn, pigs grunted as they shifted, cows called to calves, chickens clucked as they scratched, and the billy goat butted against his post. Today, as I listen to Gregorian chants, I recall Grampa's version, "Hup, hup, hup, easy now, hup, hup, hup," and how he lured the barn chorus from cacophony to calm, monosyllabic punctuations.

Grampa handed my fork to me and turned to load the manure spreader with his own fork. Did he smile as he turned, even just a twitch, at the corner of his mouth? I was sure I detected a pinch of pride in his face, formed firmly from a heritage of centuries of Mennonite humility. This was my fork. Of course, the handle had been broken unexpectedly and it was a three-pronged pitch fork instead of a multi-pronged manure fork. Nevertheless, the handle was sanded where my upper hand gripped and it was exactly my height.

I fixed my eye on a soft clump of cattle manure, stabbed, and heaved it into the spreader. The slightly delayed plop assured me my effort was effective. The sharp smell of ammonia escaped from disturbed manure, a whiff of affirmation. The spreader positioned, the chorus approving, my fork presented with quiet dignity and the work relished. God save the Queen's wave for another day.

I often think about my decision as a five-year-old when I sign research contracts as a scientist to promise Her Majesty to conduct my research as proposed and budgeted. If the truth be told, most of us who indulge in the pursuit of science are simply big curious kids who like to play. We cherish our opportunities to observe and hypothesize and test and observe and hypothesize and test again until we know a little bit more, within a level of probability. It's delightful to ask, "Why does this happen or what would happen if … ?" The rest of you should be thankful we are quirky enough to think we're having fun and thus carry on with repetitive trials and detailed analysis.

Nevertheless, in spite of our closeted playfulness, agricultural scientists are dead serious when speaking or writing to justify research protocols. There is no thought of waiting for another day; our deliberate wave, our salute to the Queen and society, is our essential, perpetual service. The ultimate rationale of agricultural science has been to improve the capacity for farmers to feed the world.

Perhaps it's time to relax the rigidity of our salute and ponder, like a young child, "What do we *do*, when we salute the imperative of feeding the world?"

Let's start by defining "the world." Are we planning to feed all people or only those who can pay? Do we feed only people? If so, would it be okay to deprive other beings, or even to wipe out species, so that more people can eat or so that each person can consume more? Is it acceptable to use food as a weapon by poisoning the food of enemies, or withholding it from enemies, or destroying the food-producing capacity of enemies? Feeding the world is usually a matter of producing enough food for those people living in non-hostile nations who can pay.

Water flows from high pressure to low pressure or downhill, tugged by gravity. Food flows to those with money or power. It is not the responsibility of farmers to impoverish themselves and sell their food so cheaply that it can flow to other people in poverty. While the problems that exist with distribution of food pose a barrier to addressing hunger, the distribution of money is even more limiting to those who are hungry. The wealth of 2,200 billionaires increased by $900 billion in 2018. The wealth of the richest people climbed by 12 percent; in contrast, the wealth of the poorest 3.8 billion people dropped by 11 percent. In 2018, it took only twenty-six of the top billionaires to match the wealth of half the world's population. In 2017, forty-three billionaires had to rally to accomplish the same feat (Elliot, 2019).

The billionaires, with their immense privilege, should not only allow, they should advocate for a more equitable global system of distributing wealth. If that were to happen, food security for most of the world's poor would be solved; because, if they had sufficient money, adequate amounts of food would flow to them. A world of improved food security is a more secure world for billionaires. Without a more equitable distribution of wealth, their world of privilege will be secure only until it isn't.

Most farmers rely on multinational companies to supply them with the inputs they use to grow their crops: fertilizers, pesticides, feed, electricity, fuel, machinery, building materials, computers and software, and genetic material for superior plants and animals. Farmers have incentives to produce high yields at declining per-unit costs to enhance profits. Once a farmer has made the choice to use certain kinds of inputs, it is tempting not only to continue to use these but also to increase the use of such investments to protect or build on those already made.

More than a decade ago, I served on a committee with George Brinkman, an agricultural economist, and now professor emeritus, at the University of Guelph. I recall his warnings about how farmers are exposing themselves to too much debt. A few years ago, Pilger (2014) succinctly summarized Brinkman's warning about farm viability: "Farmers in Canada are overcapitalized, and they are much more vulnerable than U.S. farmers to rising interest rates, low commodity prices, poor production, and falling land values. If prices enter a down cycle or interest rates go up, Canadian farmers will be squeezed."

Brinkman calculated the ratio of farm debt to income in Canada. In 1972, this ratio was two to one, and by 2007, that ratio had multiplied by ten and was twenty-three to one. Debt reduces options, and if someone is carrying twenty-three times as much debt as income the options available to that person will be severely reduced. The possibility of adaptation is constrained. Given all of this, it is not surprising that farmers are resistant to radical change, or in fact, to any type of change. Their position is already tenuous. Farmers have very good reasons to keep calm and carry on, hoping that markets, not to mention weather, will remain favourable and relatively consistent. Musings about how farm products ought to change to providing what people might really need are not enthusiastically entertained down on most farms. Their debts were incurred with the expectation that their current products will go to market.

Farmers are also wary of "sustainability" changes proposed by retailers to help improve "retailer green credit" with shoppers.

Too often, farmers are expected to make changes at their own expense, just to retain access to processors or retailers. If they were paid more for farm products of more sustainable practices, then farmers would be happy to embrace these better ways.

Bankers who encourage farmers to buy more land and equipment merely to produce more should consider the long-term impacts on soil health. Corn and soybean crops have a track record of repaying bankers. However, soil organic matter levels are declining (Brown, 2017). Perhaps a soil health workshop is required to help bankers understand the developing threat of their current lending practices. Dr. Wayne Honeycutt, president and CEO of the Soil Health Institute (soilhealthinstitute.org), in a 2018 visit to the University of Guelph, suggested that bankers could offer lower interest rates on loans to farmers who foster soil health. Their productive capacity will be less variable and last longer.

Agriculturalists typically respond like a hockey team to the challenge of feeding the world. With energetic skating (forward momentum), deft passing (teamwork), and well-timed checks (competitiveness), we have and will continue to win the contest against hunger. However, farmers and agricultural scientists know as clearly as anyone how precarious this venture is. Increasingly, it is becoming clearer that they are challenged with too many people, too much consumption, and too much waste. They keep putting the puck in the net and increasing food supplies with an offensive strategy. I am troubled, however, by the fact that so few agriculturalists warn about the risks of ever more consumption. There is also a need to play defence, to advocate for birth control policies, reduced consumption per person, and reduced waste per person. If consumers don't know, most of us as aggies know at some level that the long game includes defence.

Our success at adapting with technology has been striking. Hybrid corn improved yields over open-pollinated varieties early in the twentieth century, nitrogen fertilizer further advanced these gains in the mid to latter part of the same century, genetic modification followed, and precision agriculture in the early twenty-first century is seen as the adaptation that will address the threat of too little food.

However, clouds hover. Soil erosion, fossil-fuel dependence, decline of water supplies, air pollution, and less stable weather patterns are affecting farmers' potential to produce food. While all of these developments have serious implications, it might be useful to view them as not simply threats. They can be seen, too, as blessings. It's possible to view these developments as messages from Gaia, sent to help remind us about the biological limits of the world. Rather than seeking technological advances that enable us to grow more food, we should adopt a different, better strategy: accept living with less fuel, less consumption per person, less waste per person; and plan for less people, in an economy that is dynamically stable, while designed to avoid the perils of unsustainable growth.

Feeding the world involves providing people with sufficient calories and protein and minerals for health and stability. But it's necessary to look at what people eat, and how much, if we are to feed them while maintaining their health and Earth's health. What can we do if consumers are abdicating food awareness?

Companies with food for sale want customers to repeatedly buy their products. They want to please shareholders, and the most common way to do that is to sell as much food as possible while producing that food as cheaply as possible. Satisfying the cravings of their customers, the makers of processed food create products that sell because of their sweetness, because of their saltiness. Ingredients are expertly mixed into unique and instantly appealing products.

These ingredients are sourced from farms as commodities — grains, oilseeds, milk, meat, and produce. Agricultural corporations sell patented inputs to farmers, prudently purchase commodities at low prices, and break apart and reassemble food products to appeal to the hardwired desires of consumers, to optimize profits.

And farmers grow the crops used in these products and sell their crops and animals to agricultural corporations. To be fair to farmers, many of them have worked long hours and invested large sums to produce the food that they do. Despite that, they have received low returns for their efforts in the last few decades. Can we blame farmers for being enthused about the possibility of selling more — to those who want to consume more or to the more mouths who will need more food? This opportunity seems long overdue for the struggling farmers who have subsidized the plenty for people's palates with their sweat and investments.

Farmers justifiably resist admonitions to produce food sustainably. After all, the cost would be theirs. Urban consumers, who are now adding their desire that food be sustainable to their current demands for choice and the convenience of cheap food, would get all of the benefits. To secure food supplies consumers could share responsibility for production variability and risks. In the twenty-first century and beyond, the old model of feeding the world, farmers feeding consumers, will not suffice. This "us" and "them" approach, with food as the currency, shifts the emphasis to products, profit, and power. Our present food system is feeding, or more accurately supplying (often in excess), those who can pay for it. Others are food insecure, with attendant health costs. This theme is developed more in chapter 5.

But food is more than a mere commodity, to be bought, sold, and consumed. Food, like water and oxygen, is essential and should be seen as a public good, available to all. This is not to say that an economy of growing, processing, distributing, and retailing food must be eliminated. However, this economy should be focused on sustainability and social justice rather than focused inordinately on market opportunities for large companies and on growing profits for them. A healthy society, where commerce flourishes along with arts, education, health, and other sectors, needs adequately fed citizens. A society that fails to provide nutritious, affordable food grown in a sustainable way fails as a society. It is that simple.

Many aggies proudly display bumper stickers declaring "Farmers Feed Cities" or "No Farms, No Food." The sense of pride captured in these bumper stickers is allied with a kind of defensiveness. These truths should be so obvious as to not need mentioning. There is a realization among farmers, however, that a social licence is needed for agriculture to flourish — or at least for farmers to flourish. Trust between city-dwellers and those working on farms needs to be established. There needs to be respect, too. The "city mouse" stories of the "country mouse" sting.

"Today cities are crucibles of ingenuity and productivity generating more than 80 percent of the world's patents and about 80 percent of global gross domestic product (GDP). Urban dwellers tend to be happier, healthier, better educated and more prosperous than their rural counterparts" (Muggah, 2017).

Muggah's observation invites the question, why don't we all move to cities? I recall a wizened refugee from the GTA, who had retired in Muskoka, sighing in relief and saying, "I'm happy that so many people want to live in Toronto. Then I don't have to."

Across the globe more than half the human population has been living in cities for at least ten years. According to the 2016 census, more than one-third of Canadians now live in just three cities: Toronto, Montreal, and Vancouver. About 82 percent of Canucks reside in large- and medium-sized cities. The average age in rural areas is rising faster than in cities, and immigrants, many of them of a younger demographic, are drawn to cities.

Richard Florida and colleagues (2015) at the Martin Prosperity Institute, Rotman School of Management, University of Toronto, propose that there is an emergent class — knowledge workers, intellectuals, and various types of artists — that has become the dominant economic force. The rise of this class coincides with an economic shift that has devalued the products of agriculture and industry and has brought about a general restructuring of affairs and more complex economic hierarchies in cities.

Florida and his colleagues argue that the Global Creativity Index (GCI) is a "broad-based measure for advanced economic growth and sustainable prosperity based on the 3Ts of economic development — talent, technology, and tolerance." In 2015, Canada ranked first in tolerance and fourth overall. "Creativity is also closely connected to urbanization, with more urbanized nations scoring higher on the GCI."

Does this mean that creativity in the countryside is deficient? The picture that emerges if one looks at the averages of various measurements is a disturbing one. My observations of the people I know or have come into contact with in rural Canada have shown me, however, that there is an immense amount of creativity, grounded in common sense, there. For example, a farm couple near Thunder Bay successfully raise sheep in a habitat of wolves, coyotes, and bears. They have designed a unique, cost-effective electric fence that does a fine job of keeping predators out — a bit of support from occasional live rounds fired from the front porch is sometimes needed. Lamb sales are humming and the predators have to balance their diets with wild prey.

Technology is being adopted in farming, forestry, and fishing, three of the basic industries that helped this country grow, just as quickly as it is happening in the city. And, believe me, the people adopting new technologies are doing much more than simply learning how to operate equipment as it comes off the shelf. Check out a farm machine shop some day when you have an inspiration deficit. It can take a big dash of ingenuity after hours of practise and observation and dollops of patience and perseverance to rig up a new machine to do the job properly. Bright, young, practical farmers are talented at adopting technologies to improve economic opportunities and prosperity in rural sectors.

However, as in urban areas, automation is displacing rural people who are skilled in traditional tasks. Wendell Berry has advocated for a higher eyes-to-acres ratio. His warning is that more machinery and sensors will not adequately replace old-fashioned observations and inferences. The challenge is to keep rural people engaged with their eyes, synthesizing proficiencies, relational awareness, and respectful attitudes. How do we notice what is really happening and adjust, as required?

> The standards of our behavior must be derived, not from the capability of technology, but from the nature of places and communities. We must shift the priority from production to local adaptation, from innovation to familiarity, from power to elegance, from costliness to thrift. We must learn to think about propriety in scale and design, as determined by human and ecological health. By such changes we might again make our work an answer to despair. (Berry, 2000)

Research conducted in biological systems without synthetic inputs, under organic methods, reveals relationships and interactions sometimes not observed under conditions of high synthetic inputs. Research in organic systems often boosts efficiency in non-organic systems as well. For example, organic farmers have been correctly challenged by their neighbours about the need for too much tillage. Given that synthetic herbicides are not allowed in organic systems it was deemed impossible to control weeds without tillage. I was regularly chided as an organic researcher for promoting diesel-fuel farming and too much tillage because I continued to investigate ways to control weeds without synthetic herbicides. That was until a Mennonite farmer in Pennsylvania built a roller crimper, a cylinder with angled blades running along the outside in a pressure-maximizing chevron curve, that achieves 90–100 percent termination of rye cover crops in one pass (Moyer, 2011).

The roller crimper achieves a number of goals unavailable through other termination methods, like those employing mowers. It lays down a cover crop neatly and evenly and crushes the mature stems without severing them. This means that the residues remain in place when the tractor passes during planting and in extreme weather. Crimping the cover crop perpendicularly, or at an angle to the cover crop rows, further prevents within-row gaps in the mulch. A no-till drill can be used to plant the following cash crop into the laid-down mulch and the cash crop success depends strongly on the cover crop ability to suppress weeds (Beach et al., 2018).

Over the last decade, with research support, more farmers are practising reduced tillage with roller crimpers. Howard G. Buffett, author of the book *Forty Chances*, still farms with pesticides, as he deems necessary, but, given he has the genes of his father, Warren, he assesses the roller crimper to be very cost effective.

> [T]here is a smaller, sturdy, low-tech implement … that we are starting to believe may have more potential, pound for pound, to help poor, fragile farmers feed their families than big tractors and planters can. It's not fancy or shiny and our guys welded modifications to the original design themselves…. It's called a roller crimper, and it looks like an oversized

> kitchen rolling pin with a raised-pattern sur-
> face.… [I]t kills cover crops without chemi-
> cals. It can be scaled up to a 60 foot rig, pulled
> by a large tractor, or scaled down to be pulled
> by oxen.

Some non-organic squash and pumpkin farmers in Ontario started using the roller crimper on a rye cover crop before seeding their large gourds. Now retailers are asking more farmers to use this "organic" technique, because, by resting on the mulch, the squash stays cleaner, without a flat spot, in contrast to dirtier squash with flat spots, on bare ground. Non-organic farmers are lining up to check out the cost savings, aesthetic appeal, and ecological benefits for other cash crops, including corn and soybean.

Returning to the concept of the Global Creativity Index, Florida says that the GCI scores Canada as the top country in tolerance, with the implication that our cities boosted us to the summit. Perhaps some aspects of tolerance do improve as varying types of people continuously rub elbows in cities. They learn to accept each other and get on with the tasks at hand, especially when there are plenty of tasks to manage in a wealthy nation's economy.

However, some of us also appreciate that rural resilience and the relationships of rural people with other people, as well as animals, plants, and ecosystems, are being negatively affected by the constant demand for the transfer of resources beyond what rural Canada can realistically sustain. And then there is the fact that talented rural youth are often forced to move to urban areas to find work. The drain on rural people and resources is enormous.

Cities are seductive magnets. And yet, the future of civilization still hinges on the observations, relationships, and actions of engaged rural realists. It is mostly in rural areas that layers of leaves photosynthesize to convert sunlight energy, and where clean water and healthy soil are the foundation of food and fibre production.

The 18 percent remaining in rural Canada support the rest of us in ways we are slow to appreciate. To sustain happy, healthy, well-educated, and prosperous urbanites requires the awareness, skills, creativity, and even tolerance of rural stalwarts, with the understanding to harvest sustainably. The 82 percent who are urbanites will do well to adjust their consumption to what is adequate.

5

FOOD AND HEALTH

Two-thirds of direct health-care costs and 60 percent of indirect health-care costs in Canada can now be attributed to chronic diseases (e.g., cancer, cardiovascular conditions, diabetes) associated with unhealthy eating (Dubé et al., 2009). Despite the critical role that food plays in our nutrition and overall health, food is not widely seen or consumed as medicine. This oversight has dire consequences. Health, or perhaps more aptly "sickness," budgets continue to ratchet upwards. If we prioritized health, then food would be valued and consumed for prevention of illness, thus reducing costs for treating those who eat poorly.

The U.S. food industry spends $2 billion per year to market to children. This is a huge amount and pays for a massive amount of advertising. It is little wonder, then, given the typical viewing habits of children, that the average U.S. child, in 2011, watched and absorbed twelve to sixteen television ads per day for food or drinks. Most of the products so advertised were high in saturated fat, sugar, or sodium (Yale Rudd Centre, 2013). In Canada, the Heart and Stroke Foundation (2017) reported that our youngest citizens (ages two to eleven) spend eight hours per day in front of screens and in one year view more than twenty-five million food and beverage ads. Over 90 percent of these pitches are for unhealthy foods. Their bolded sidebar statement, "Industry should pick on someone its own age," nails the issue. Talk about David versus Goliath. At least David had a slingshot to defend himself. Our children are more like David's lambs. Why do we keep enabling Goliath when our innocents are defenceless?

You obviously didn't listen to your mother if you don't know that you should eat your vegetables. To assess whether food company executives had listened to their moms, Children Now, a national advocacy group for children's issues, commissioned an assessment of the Children's Food and Beverage Advertising Initiative in December 2009. They determined that ads for fruits, vegetables, and whole grains were almost non-existent, at less than 1 percent of total ads from participating companies. The other 99 percent of ads were for foods with low to moderate nutritional value (ChangeLab Solutions, 2012).

It's important to provide our emerging generation with some defence against direct and subliminal effects of advertising. When my daughter was a toddler, and I was a hawk-eyed parent, TV generally and advertising in particular were offensive to me. In an attempt to instill the same values in my daughter that I held, I devised a game for us to play: we would not buy anything we saw advertised on the bit of TV we watched. She held me to it and we were richer for it. She would admonish me when she caught me selecting a branded item, possibly one that I had been buying long before she arrived, but that she had seen advertised. Two decades later, she remains a skeptic of advertising and avoids soft drinks. I am a lucky man.

This is not to say we should let Goliath off the hook. Our current zeitgeist may be unduly influenced by Windigo, the legendary monster of Algonquian-speaking First Nations in North America. The Windigo, which is born of our fears and failings, is that part "within us which cares more for its own survival than for anything else" (Kimmerer, 2013). What within us accepts that our survival depends on higher sales and greater economic returns, even when we know they facilitate some predator companies that exploit and harm our most vulnerable?

In the U.S., the carbonated soft drink (CSD) segment of soft drink companies spent $492 million on marketing. The kicker is that $474 million, or 96 percent, was advertising specifically for adolescents, ages twelve to seventeen. At shareholder meetings, the stated goal of these companies is to leverage the spending power of kids with pocket money and to build brand loyalty early. Past business experience indicates this brand loyalty will be carried through to adulthood (ChangeLab Solutions, 2012). How do corporate social responsibility policy makers rationalize such specific, predatory targeting of youth?

In the last forty years, the treat of enjoying soda in the U.S. has tripled for boys and doubled for girls. Young males ages twelve to twenty-nine gulp over 160 gallons per year, or about two litres per young person per day (Global Healing Centre, 2016). The title of the Global Healing Centre's report, "Soft Drinks: America's Other Drinking Problem," proclaims the fact that what many see as a relatively harmless indulgence — a simple snack — has morphed into an addiction, an addiction the soft drink companies want to continue for lifetimes, in order to please their executives and shareholders.

> Soft drink companies do engage in corporate social responsibility by donating to initiatives such as after school programs, parks and rail to trail organizations. However some advocates fear that these philanthropic endeavors are "buying silence" in the health community. For example, Save the Children, a group that works on children's health issues in the U.S. and around the world, ended its involvement in sugar sweetened beverage (SSB) tax campaigns around the same time that the organization sought a grant from Coca-Cola for education programs. (ChangeLab Solutions, 2012)

> Branding often involves retelling the same fictional story again and again, until people become convinced it is the truth. What images come to mind when you think about Coca-Cola? Do you think about healthy young people engaging in sports and having fun together? Or do you think about overweight diabetes patients lying in a hospital bed? (Harari, 2018)

In a struggle that goes back at least to my undergrad days in the 1970s, milk formula companies have been promoting their products for infants. Breast milk, a liquid that differs in every way from soft drinks, except that they are both wet, is also a target for food industry manipulation. In July 2018, a U.S. delegation to the U.N. was adamant that the phrase "protect, promote and support breast-feeding" be omitted from an international health promotion resolution (Pilkington, 2018). Why would the government of the world's largest economy take this step and, furthermore, imply that it might cut its annual contribution ($845 million) to the World Health Organization if other countries didn't acquiesce? The milk formula industry, which is based in the United States (and Europe), knows its sales are stagnating. Although their annual take is still $70 billion, they lobbied for assistance. Numerous studies have shown the benefits of breastfeeding, including one at Harvard in 2016 that "estimated that 3,340 premature deaths a year among both mothers and babies could be prevented in the US alone given adequate breastfeeding" (Pilkington, 2018). Is there any more compelling evidence that Windigo still strides stupidly, caring more for its own monstrous survival — the creation of greater profits for corporations — than for anything else?

It has been reported that a substantial subsample of the species *Homo sapiens* is frequently observed grazing on long, skinny, white french fries. Apparently, these upright potato parallelograms are plucked, dripping with a sugar and tomato substance, from colourful boxes, without the customary humanoid utensils. A dietary advantage is not detectable and thus is unlikely to be the driving factor for this fickle feeding frenzy.

The health implications to agro-ecological systems of this dubious staple are increasingly of concern. They are one of the major food sources of acrylamide. Studies in rodent models have found that acrylamide exposure increases the risk for several types of cancer (National Cancer Institute, 2017). French fries, along with other types of fried potatoes, increase our risk of premature mortality over the years (Walton, 2017).

To make long, skinny, white french fries, processors are paying a premium to farmers for large Russet Burbank potatoes. Farmers grow what is profitable. The white colour of Russet Burbanks and the bulked-up size and shape of these tubers, which allow a relatively greater number of lengthy fries to be cut from them, make them just the ticket for processors seeking to meet the demands of this peculiar market.

Large tubers are not natural. To grow bulked-up tubers, farmers are encouraged to apply excessive amounts of nitrogen fertilizer, a product requiring unusually high energy inputs to manufacture. The use of nitrogen-rich fertilizers has been designed to provide easy nitrogen access to the tubers. However, the extra nitrogen fertilizer not taken up by plants in wet, late-season soils, can transform to nitrous oxide, a greenhouse gas three hundred times more potent than carbon dioxide. Nitrogen fertilizer remaining in soil also transforms to nitrate, leaches into groundwater and becomes toxic at concentrations above ten parts per million, leading to blue baby syndrome.

To optimize the potential of Russet Burbank potatoes (140 days from seeding to harvest) to attain maximum size, they are harvested as late as possible. In PEI potato country, a late harvest is one in October. By then, the window has shut for establishing a cover crop to suck up the remaining nitrogen fertilizer not used by potatoes. The lack of a cover crop leaves the disturbed soil exposed to erosive wind gusts (up to ninety kilometres per hour) in the fall and winter and to erosive running water after snowmelt the next spring.

As the potato season lengthens, there is also a higher risk of potatoes being infected with blight, the same disease associated with the Irish potato famine. Fungicides are increasingly applied to prevent or contain blight as harvest is delayed, with concomitant stresses on ground water quality and human health.

Some farmers, including Matt Ramsay, a member of the Kensington North Watershed Association on PEI, are experimenting with establishing cereal rye as a cover crop. They broadcast the rye seed at high rates of 175 to 200 pounds per acre about five to seven days before potatoes are dug. The potato digging equipment buries some of the rye seed too deeply for germination after potato harvest. Nevertheless, a good portion does germinate and provides some cover to protect the soil from late-season winds and spring water runoff. Matt explains that success of the cover crop is improved if the potato harvest is earlier.

An earlier harvest of smaller potatoes would reduce the problems of applying excess fertilizer and fungicides and leaving the potato field bare after harvest. In fact, organic potato production, without synthetic fertilizer and pesticides, and with cover crops, is becoming more common with smaller potatoes, harvested earlier.

The Little Potato Company (littlepotatoes.com) is specializing in growing and processing small creamer potatoes. The ecological footprint of this product is much smaller than that of the hefty potatoes grown for fries.

Roger Henry, an agronomist at the PEI Harrington research station of Agriculture and Agri-Food Canada, notes that "the ideal potato variety for fries would grow in the shape of a brick, in less than one hundred days." Until such a variety is available, we might rethink our long, skinny, white fry habit.

More than half of Canadian adults are now overweight or obese (Dubé et al., 2009), but each year we still nibble a quarter of a million tonnes of french fries (Statista, 2018). It's common knowledge that baked, roasted, and boiled potatoes are healthier choices than fried potatoes. The risk of catching a cold or flu is also higher when eating with our fingers.

The long, skinny, white fry trend may have been acceptable when we didn't know any better. Now we do, so it's time to drop this bad habit.

An insightful research project in Ontario by Valerie Tarasuk and her team linked food insecurity to health costs. Contrasted with the health cost of those living in food-secure households, annual health-care costs are up to 23 percent higher in households with marginal food insecurity, 49 percent higher in households with moderate food insecurity, and 121 percent higher in households with severe food insecurity (Tarasuk et al., 2015). Not surprisingly, the researchers concluded: "Policy interventions at the provincial or federal level designed to reduce household food insecurity could offset considerable public expenditures in health care."

I must confess that this paper confirmed my biases about food security and health. As an aside, let me be clear that as a scientist I have biases and I'm sure all scientists do, whether acknowledged or not. It is appropriate to recognize this human proclivity and to be willing to test against a bias. We organize our thoughts according to how we understand the world and develop hypotheses that require testing. If my experiments show that I am wrong or that more research scrutiny is required, then so be it.

I believe that reducing the costs of healthy food would help those living with significant food insecurity. I was determined to test a hypothesis that would show the viability of one of the policy options that could achieve this goal. However, I learned after several attempts to secure funding to test a potential policy option about food and health that it was not attractive to funding institutions. My colleagues and I hypothesized that it is cheaper to provide free Ontario fruits and vegetables for all low-income citizens in Ontario than it is to keep paying increasing marginal health costs that can be attributed to their current diet. However, we never did get funding for the research.

Our research team consisted of me and Drs. Michael Von Massow, Rong Cao, and Laura Forbes. In our proposal, which was written mostly by Dr. Von Massow, we wrote:

> Our objective is to establish whether there is long-term societal value in providing access to free fruits and vegetables for food insecure individuals. Food insecure individuals have been shown to be at greater risk for chronic

diseases, including diabetes, obesity and cardiovascular disease (Laraia, 2013). Diets low in vegetables and fruit among food insecure individuals may explain this relationship. Access to fruits and vegetables has been identified as a particular problem in food insecure households (Bruening et al., 2012) and data from the Canadian Community Health Survey shows that individuals who were food insecure had significantly lower vegetable and fruit intakes compared to food secure individuals (Kirkpatrick and Tarasuk, 2008). Previous studies have evaluated the impact of communication and education on fruit and vegetable consumption behaviours. For example, there have been evaluations of the impact of improved nutrition information (Bartels and van den Berg, 2011; Herbert et al., 2010), of appealing to vanity (Whitehead et al., 2012), product placement (Sigurdsson, Larsen, and Gunnarsson, 2010) and of psychological factors such as subjective self well-being and others (Ding et al., 2014; Umeh and Sharps, 2012) on fruit and vegetable purchasing intentions or behaviour.

However, the above studies have no explicit measure of fruit and vegetable consumption; therefore true compliance has not been assessed. In order for the intervention to be truly effective, individuals have to actually consume more fresh fruits and vegetables to achieve the associated health benefits. Understanding the specific responses and level of compliance is critical in order to quantify the benefits of such an intervention. We believe our study would be the first to attempt to measure actual compliance in order to identify the value associated with such a specific policy intervention.

Eating fruits and vegetables may be the ultimate expression of radical independence. They are relatively inexpensive and available fresh, in large quantities, for several months each year. There are well-known methods to preserve fruits and vegetables for winter consumption. With a small plot of land, they can be grown by families, and small enterprises can cultivate them also, providing several options to buy or trade for them. They are not a scarce commodity, and there is absolutely no justification for having the distribution and sale of them dominated by large food processors and retailers, which extract hard-earned cash for their provision. With only a few small changes to the system it would be possible to access fruits and vegetables without the food industry. We would all be healthier for it.

I understand that today a single mom on a low income may have to choose to use limited funds to make sure her children have sufficient calories, before spending on fruits and vegetables. I understand that many do not have the knowledge and skills necessary to grow, harvest, store, and prepare food. All the more reason to be sure that food awareness and skills become part of the education curriculum from Kindergarten to Grade

12. Teaching these subjects in school would help ensure that all parents and all householders of the future can enjoy this slice of self-reliance.

Food banks were at first expected to be temporary. Now, about forty years after the opening of the first ones, and spending on infrastructure, there seems to be acceptance that they are here to stay and that an ongoing commitment is required. For example, the California Association of Food Banks needs more than $150 million for infrastructure upgrading. What if the money spent on maintaining food banks was, instead, allocated to hungry people for the specific purpose of buying the food they need, when they need it, at retail outlets closest to where they already live?

We use credit and debit cards for many purchases. We could issue cards that have the allotted funds on them. There is technology available to ensure that those receiving funds would be able to use such cards only for food. Card readers could be used at farmers' markets and all other retail outlets. Could food banks use their volunteers more effectively if their task was to assign monthly reloadable cards to folks in need? If so, relatively little food bank infrastructure would be required.

To date, the federal and Ontario governments have not picked up the responsibility to directly provide food to hungry citizens. Should it be left to food banks to discern immediate food needs and to make food available? This is not an easy task in Canada, where poverty is often hidden, yet stubbornly persists for about 10 percent of the population. Access to tax records would clarify the process.

The card system, described above, would have the advantage of offering privacy; users would not be easily distinguished from regular card users. While this card system would not be universal nor an answer for all of the problems affecting those unable to purchase sufficient healthy food, it could help to maintain the dignity of users, granting them anonymity, while at the same time addressing the real-time needs of many.

To enable everyone to have access to fruits and vegetables and other healthy food, we must address poverty. Like Hugh Segal, a former senator, now master of Massey College, I am an advocate for a guaranteed annual income (GAI), sometimes referred to as a universal basic income (UBI) policy, in Canada. It can be seen as a negative tax system: families and individuals below the poverty threshold would be paid a monthly amount to raise their income to the level required for an acceptable standard of living. In Canada, hunger is a function of poverty, rather than of food scarcity. A guaranteed annual income could effectively address hunger.

In a trial program that ran from 1974 to 1978, all citizens of Dauphin, Manitoba, were provided with a guaranteed annual income. This trial showed that there was almost no reduction in hours worked, except among women who chose to stay home with young children, elderly parents, or disabled family members. I was surprised and thrilled to learn recently that my uncle Adin served as a social worker in Dauphin during this experiment.

Hugh Segal points out that it would actually be more cost-effective for federal and provincial governments to fund a national GAI policy than to carry on with the plethora of programs to assist people with disabilities, job losses, marriage breakdowns, and other propellants to poverty. Current programs require excessive administration and only partially alleviate poverty.

Drs. Noralou Roos and Evelyn Forget of the Fraser Institute, not a flaming left-wing outpost, back up Segal's claims with impressive data. To implement a GAI program as per the Dauphin protocol would have cost $17 billion, in Canada, in 2015. To go all the way to a Cadillac luxury GAI would have cost $58 billion. In contrast, the total cost of Canada's current income support system (payout plus administration costs) was $185 billion in 2013.

Imagine, as an example of low-income people, how single moms of the future might feel more empowered with a GAI (while not having to keep explaining their need for cash) and a suite of food skills they had learned throughout their school years. It's not difficult to further imagine that they and their children might be healthier and happier and more engaged in contributing their human capacity to society.

(Although perhaps not practicable for most people now, particularly those living in apartments in cities, it might be possible in the future that with a GAI and availability of information ordinary people could grow and preserve at least some of their own food. As a child I recall the mystery of creeping down the old farmhouse stairs into the cellar and then pulling the string to the single light bulb, which illuminated a burst of primary colours from jars of peaches, beets, tomatoes, applesauce, beans, and even homemade ketchup. It would be a great boon if more people today and in the future could share that joy … and the nutritional benefits, too.)

A GAI can provide benefits other than an improved standard of living (and the improved health that accompanies that). It can also help individuals live a spiritually richer life.

Siddhartha, an ascetic Brahmin in the story composed by Hermann Hesse, chooses to expand his understanding of life by approaching a merchant to learn his trade (Hesse, 2000). The skeptical merchant criticizes Siddhartha for living off the wealth of others. Siddhartha notes that the merchant does, too. The merchant then asks Siddhartha what he has to offer in exchange for training. Siddhartha says, "I can think, I can wait and I can fast." Suffice it to say that, over time, Siddhartha's skills multiply the business of the merchant. However, after two decades, Siddhartha chooses to return to a simple life and to listen to a river with a still heart and an open soul.

In the fast-paced modern world we live in, with its emphasis on chasing money, trinkets, and electronic distractions, we might all benefit from a GAI system, since it would allow us all to spend time on things that benefit the soul: contemplation, art, philosophy, music, and theatre, at selected life stages. We need time and room in our lives to develop an attitude of gratitude, and to attend more closely to our food.

A lifestyle of scrambling leads to accepting food industry provisions of processed food, seductive because of its convenience and its appeal to our love of the salty and the sweet, but offering minimal nutritional value. In addition to paying dearly to give up our food independence, we eat food as if a meal is just one of several other tasks we must manage simultaneously.

Food is much more than a product. It connects us viscerally to Earth. Food is medicine and food is the foundation of our health.

6

WASTED FOOD AND ATTENDANT LOSSES

I crawled up the ladder to the higher branches of the Snow Apple tree for the umpteenth time. My pail wasn't large and this time I didn't want to fill it too quickly. My hand followed my eye to the choicest apple within reach. I plucked, swiveled my flexible eight-year-old body on the ladder, leaned back against the top rung, and chomped. The sweet taste filled my mouth. Below, my cousins and siblings were climbing and stooping to pick and then pour apples into bags for the apple-butter haul to Wellesley.

I noticed my uncle Addison approaching my tree, so I took another quick bite, tossed the half-eaten apple and got back to work.

"Were you eating this apple?" he asked a moment later. Yup, he was pointing to my apple.

I nodded.

"Come on down, pick it up, and finish it."

"But there are so many apples all over this orchard and they're going for apple butter anyway."

"That doesn't matter. If you start to eat a perfectly good apple, then eat it all. In our family we don't waste."

I never forgot that lesson.

We waste 40 percent of our food in Canada, at an annual cost of $31 billion. This waste is 2 percent of Canada's GDP and more than the total GDP of the thirty-two poorest countries in the world (Gooch and Felfel, 2014). Furthermore, Gooch and Felfel note, the "cumulative cost of associated wastes (energy, water, land, labour, capital investment, infrastructure, machinery, transport, etc.) is about two and a half times greater than the 'face value' of wasted food. Thus, the overall annual cost of wasted food in Canada exceeds $100 billion."

In a more recent research report, the same team (Gooch et al., 2019), reported that $49.5 billion, i.e., 3 percent of Canada's 2016 GDP, which could feed everybody in Canada for five months, is the value of *avoidable* food loss and waste (FLW) in Canada. Notice, this is only the avoidable FLW (e.g., bruised apples, which people avoid eating). An example of unavoidable wasted food is an apple core — unavoidable waste maybe, but since the apple lesson I received from my uncle, the apple cores that I throw away have no edible flesh and are much smaller than the apple cores I see being tossed in lunchrooms. Most people assume eggshells are unavoidable wasted food, but I have a friend who includes boiled and finely ground egg shells in smoothies, to supplement her calcium. I was very aware, when evaluating the amount of wasted food from curbside containers in Guelph, that there was a mushy middle between avoidable and unavoidable wasted food.

My uncle Addison and others who lived through the Depression knew about valuing and respecting food. They understood that an attitude of gratitude for what we have is demonstrated by the many small actions we make to prevent waste.

A few years after my apple lesson, I began participating in 4-H projects that focused on growing corn and raising beef cattle. Then, as now, most involved in production agriculture believed that since the global population is growing we must plan for how we can responsibly feed the extra people that will soon inhabit the planet. What was left out of the discussions then and is still left out of most discussions on the subject today is the fact that there would be little problem feeding additional people if more of the food that is produced were actually eaten. Farmers aren't the only ones who can make a contribution to solving the problem of hunger. If consumers wasted less food, then farmers would have less pressure to produce more.

An aside. Sometimes I need feedback from another person to help me learn something that I thought I knew. On one occasion, after I gave a talk about food waste — I'm sure the term was in the title of my talk — one of the members of the audience rose and challenged me: "Why is it food waste, as if food, as an adjective, is referring to just another type of waste? Shouldn't we talk about wasted food with the emphasis on food as the noun? Food is not really comparable to other waste." I acknowledged the wisdom of this admonishment immediately and have been referring to wasted food ever since.

Across the globe, one billion extra people could be fed if we applied the best current methods to reduce wasted food (Kummu et al., 2012). I urge you to look again at the adjective "current." These are not methods of the future, waiting to be developed. In fact, these are methods already in place. What is required is that we simply implement what is now done to achieve the lowest loss and waste percentages achieved in any region, in each step of the food supply chain. We could do this now if we applied what we know. More than half of the losses are inefficiencies of distribution and consumption in middle- and high-income countries; in low-income countries, the main losses are realized during agricultural and post-harvest processes.

Perhaps we are hardwired to consume or hoard as much food as we can, in case we encounter famine or hunger. We can, however, learn to overcome our tendency to gluttony and waste, and then take the remainder and store it in a manner so that it retains its food value.

In our hectic lives, there is a temptation to act as if we are too busy to worry about how much food we buy. It's second nature to buy large quantities of food, especially if that food is advertised as being "on sale," even if we realize some will not actually be consumed. Many fridges in Canada are jammed with good food and then cleaned out to make room for the next batch of groceries. We consume only some of the food stored before each purge. Those who use only one or two criteria, such as appearance or smell, to assess whether or not to keep food, waste less food than those who typically have multiple reasons to discard food (Parizeau, Von Massow, and Martin, 2015). Eating meals away from home, at the last minute, rather than eating at home as planned, is another factor that contributes to wasting food at home. Those who spend more money on non-grocery food from restaurants, take-outs, cafeterias, etc. spend more money on food at home and waste more food at home, apparently because of bad planning (Parizeau, Von Massow, and Martin, 2015).

It's not only consumers who waste food. "Industry's culture of accepting FLW (particularly that which occurs in the home) extends to some businesses and organizations [which view] FLW as a benefit to industry, because it drives increased sales" (Gooch et al., 2019).

Our wasted food research at the University of Guelph revealed that 85 percent of the Guelph citizens we interviewed felt guilty about wasting food; it was also discovered that the more guilty people felt, the less food they were likely to waste (Parizeau, Von Massow, and Martin, 2015). Perhaps guilt is not the most desired motivation for reducing wasted food, and yet it appears to help us prevent the profligacy of overprovisioning.

Healthy food is the stuff of life. It is worth taking time to plan food purchases to ensure that what is purchased is necessary for the meals that we intend to prepare. Taking care when shopping for food can make a real contribution to preventing wasted food, thus ensuring that we have a sustainable food system.

The majority of food wastage occurs as we go about our regular lives, but it happens at other times, too. I had never considered this, but one of my students showed me that this is true — my students teach me in ways they may never realize. This student volunteered to do a project on wasted food because she wanted to learn more about it. I'm sure she will be assigned a special place in academic heaven. In the end, she reviewed the ways in which all major religions end up wasting food. Not surprisingly, all the religious groups she studied proclaimed that humans have a moral obligation to prevent the waste of food. What surprised me was that most of these religious groups admitted, perhaps sheepishly, that their religious feasts were occasions when a significant amount of food is wasted. No doubt there is a spiritual scholar somewhere studying how to praise and celebrate while being prudent with food at feasts.

Wasting food results in the waste of other resources, too. On a global basis, the food supplies that are lost and wasted account for 12 to 15 percent of fresh water that humans directly consume and 24 percent of fresh water used in food crop production (Kummu et al., 2012). As fresh water supplies become scarcer, such losses will have increasingly negative impacts on food production and on the environment. This will result in greater human suffering. Of course, there will be political and economic implications, too.

By way of contrast, if food were not lost nor wasted around the world, as an estimated reference scenario to demonstrate relative potential, then 23 percent more total global cropland could be available and total global fertilizer use could be reduced by 23 percent. In addition, by reducing avoidable losses and waste of food we could reduce GHG emissions by 22 percent (Gooch et al., 2019). The proportion of food produced that becomes FLW, is the same proportion of energy used for food production, processing, and transportation that is wasted along with the food not utilized. Similarly, FLW is responsible for that proportion of biodiversity losses related to agricultural production. The proportion of FLW is a lost opportunity to otherwise improve soil quality, reduce labour, save money, and enhance future food production capacity and resilience. To consciously prevent wastage of food is to demonstrate an enlarged respect for food and its vital role in our survival and connection to Earth.

When I was a kid in 4-H in the 1960s, there were about 3.5 billion humans on the planet and by now we have more than doubled our numbers to beyond 7.6 billion. For the most part, farmers have been amazingly effective at producing enough food.

Some say the story is the same today. More people require more food and so we must produce it. I contend that the food equation is more complicated than that. It is true that the amount of food we require is a function of how many people live on Earth. However, the amount of required food is also determined by consumption per person and by waste per person. Most respondents in our research survey agreed that wasting food is first a social problem and then an economic or environmental problem (Parizeau, Von Massow, and Martin, 2015). Overall, the total required food equals the number of people multiplied by consumption per person plus waste per person. Although estimates vary, an average Canadian within our social context and culture goes through several times as much food as an average Bangladeshi.

In North America, each person, on average, has 3,660 calories of food available for consumption, each day (Roser and Ritchie, 2017). An average healthy person requires less than

2,300 calories per day, so we have an available excess of 1.6 times more food energy per person than we need.

Farmers continue to work hard to meet the demand. They are increasingly challenged with unexpected weather events as a result of a shifting climate and less stable economic conditions.

What is the Canadian consumer's role in the food equation? Obviously, eating the appropriate amount of food will put less stress on ourselves and on the ecosystem from which food is derived. We can also improve our health by eating real food that is well-balanced with calories, protein, vitamins, and minerals. How much high-fructose corn syrup do we need in soft drinks and snacks? To the extent that we can replace quasi-food with healthy food, we can use our limited resources of soil, water, and energy more wisely to produce what we actually need.

Consumers can also arrest habits of wasting food. We may not set out with the intention to waste food. However, we may only shop once per week, buy plenty for the week, change our minds about menus, and then throw away produce that is no longer fresh. Perhaps we can't resist the two-for-one deals and the thrill of buying at a low price. Another way to think about the food we buy is to calculate the price per 100 grams of healthy food that we actually eat. Research clearly shows that those who have more food awareness and who are more conscientious about food, waste less food (Parizeau, Von Massow, and Martin, 2015).

Food represents our cultural and social values and is appropriately associated with both feeling good about ourselves and the joy of being with friends and family. Food entertains us. Relationships associated with food are often deepened when the food is part of a cultural tradition. It can be fun to knowingly rise above the shallow appeal of advertisers who suggest we limit our food entertainment to glitzy, convenient food that so blatantly appeals to superficial tastes.

For the most part, in North America and Europe we remain below the replacement birth rate of 2.1 children per woman over a lifetime. In developing countries, birth rates are also decreasing in areas where poverty is addressed and, especially, where educational opportunities are increasing for girls and women. Here, we need more education pertaining to consumption per person and waste per person. Perhaps, then, we can decrease our consumption and waste parts of the food equation, too.

Jardim Gramacho, the largest landfill in the world, situated in Rio de Janeiro, is featured in the video *Waste Land*, directed by Lucy Walker. Viewing it is an eye-opening experience. Every day three thousand garbage pickers are paid to pick, sort, and assemble two hundred tonnes by hand, so that it can be recycled. "It's a bit like the stock market," explains one picker, "and we retrieve reusable trash that is most in demand and adjust the price according to supply."

Some are ashamed of having to resort to such degrading labour, yet others approach it with pride and recognize that about 50 percent of Rio de Janeiro's waste is being diverted from landfill and subsequent polluting effects. Even those who understand the dignity of earning a living in this way recognize that a system to divert such waste at source would be more efficient. In a world of wealthy people, too lazy to sort their trash, it is the poor who rescue them from the consequences of their negligence.

According to Valter dos Santos, vice-president of Association of Pickers, Jardim Gramacho, Rio de Janeiro, Brazil, "It's not bad to be poor. It's bad to be rich and at the height of fame, with morals that are a dirty shame."

It took an artist, Vik Muniz, to transform some of the trash to reveal its beauty. He helped the pickers to arrange the selected trash to present images of their own faces in compelling art. "When you lean in close you only see the materials but when you step back you see the image," he pointed out to the pickers. In the end, art patrons loved the results and paid handsomely for them.

About ten years ago, I met a businessman who jumped into Dumpsters at his glass company's site to get a close look at what was thrown away. In 2007, they sent 967 tonnes of waste to the landfill and by 2009 it was down to 253 tonnes. It paid to observe.

Local organizations, and people, can and do make a difference. By being proactive about finding other uses for materials already used, and sorting the used material before it goes to the landfill, we avoid having to have pickers sort through all the trash.

It pays to be aware of the materials that we no longer need and of where they are going. With just a bit of attention and extra activity we can also gain some dignity by shifting the reality of waste. Materials that are properly recycled are no longer waste, but rather resources, on the way to serving a new purpose. When those materials become art, we can even see ourselves with new insight.

❖

David Gordon, the manager of the City of Guelph Organic Waste Processing and Compost Production Facility, kindly gave a tour and answered a garbage-truck load of questions for a small group. I was struck by how thorough the designers were to prevent problems of smell and seepage. It is also a challenge to sort and manage so much organic material when citizens have tossed cigarette lighters, bottles, and other non-organic things into the compostable mix.

There is a yuck factor with organic material that many want out of their sight as soon as possible. We miss so much by not valuing compostable leftovers and scraps. Compost provides nutrients and can build soil organic matter, if properly sorted, handled, and applied to farm soils.

The lyrics of an old song are "Throw it away, where's away? There's no such place as away." The songwriter understood the problem of how he disposes of things. The stuff we don't use is still with us. If we choose to not buy what we don't need, there's less to dispose. If we choose to use what we have, as many times as possible, there's less to buy and also less to dispose. If we can no longer use something, then the trick is to recycle it.

The City of Guelph Organic Waste Processing and Compost Production Facility helped Guelph to achieve a waste diversion rate of residential waste of 69 percent in 2013. *What a great accomplishment*, I thought. However, it was explained to me that some citizens are quick to put food in the organic waste stream because they see that as a positive destination for food that is not first-rate fresh. The assumption is that if composting recycles nutrients, then surely directing food to compost is praiseworthy. Apparently organic waste per household had increased, contrasted with what it had been when it was not separated from regular garbage.

The key message or, dare I say, the first principle of addressing potentially wasted food is that we must reduce, reduce, and reduce even more how much food is wasted. That means buying no more than we can eat, whether this week or in several months. Wilted apples can go into an apple crisp. They don't have to be compost. Stale bread can be used in dressing for poultry. Appreciating and respecting food is most manifested in how we prevent its waste. Aficionados of leftovers reign supreme in the endeavor to reduce wasted food, notwithstanding a wry comment by Calvin Trillin: "The most remarkable thing about my mother is that for thirty years she served the family nothing but leftovers. The original meal has never been found."

The next option for food that we cannot consume is to make it available to other people, if at all possible. Second Harvest (secondharvest.ca) is an example of an organization that rescues food that might otherwise be unavailable to people. I am also aware that efforts are being made to assess technologies that can sterilize and preserve from plates food that is at risk of being wasted.

If food cannot be used for human consumption, then the next option in the hierarchy of food utilization is to process it for livestock feed. A Dutch company, Bonda (bonda.nl/en), adds to their feed rations co-products such as materials from the food processing sector that may not be suitable for human consumption. They thoroughly assess the origin and nutritional characteristics of these products and blend them into feed rations to optimize livestock feed utility.

A wide-awake colleague, Drew Woods, who is employed at Nutreco, an animal nutrition and feed company, has a vision of optimizing the processing of co-products that are not suitable for human consumption for animal feed. Many food processors set up shop in the Toronto region, and they are not far from livestock operations in southern Ontario. Drew is young and bright and will keep pushing until efficiencies are gained, until food is used that is currently being squandered. It makes sense to use as much human-inedible food co-product as possible to reduce the amount of land required for growing grain crops dedicated to livestock. To extend options further, one can imagine that any co-products or wasted food not suitable for livestock ingredients could be consumed by black soldier fly (*Hermetia illucens*) larvae and then, as regulations catch up, these larvae could be fed to traditional livestock (Black, 2015).

If wasted food cannot be processed for livestock, the next option, as we tumble down the stairs of how to address wasted food, is to use it for anaerobic digestion (AD), whereby both nutrients (in remaining digestate) and energy in methane can be captured. Regulations allow inclusion of up to 50 percent of on-farm feedstock from crop material, and up to 50 percent off-farm materials in the overall farm digester mix, with specific rules pertaining to allowable materials and any required pretreatments (OMAFRA, 2016). AD can offset up to 100 percent of direct energy consumption on a typical dairy farm (Main, Juhasz, and Martin, 2012). In addition, on some farms the carbon dioxide byproduct of AD can be used to enrich greenhouse air to improve efficiency of greenhouse plant photosynthesis.

Wasted food can also be used as a fuel (e.g., bioenergy) and of course it can be used as compost to recapture its nutrients. Note that AD as described above allows the capture of both energy and nutrients. However, AD infrastructure is expensive to set up in cold countries like Canada and the feedstock must be managed to be relatively consistent for the mirobes digesting it. Composting can be a cost-effective and small-scale method to recover nutrients.

There are likely other ways to divert wasted food from landfills. One might involve direct application, as a soil amendment, of the food on a field for non-food crops.

In closing this chapter, I want to contextualize wasted food. Households in Canada spend about $153 per week on food. Assuming that 20 percent of food is wasted in our households (i.e., about half of the 40 percent wasted along the value chain according to Gooch and Felfel [2014]), then the tossing cost is $31 per week. The Canada Organic Trade Association (ota.com/canada-ota) showcases information about organic food each autumn. They have noted that organic food shoppers spend $27 per week more than those who buy non-organic food. For those who now buy non-organic food and waste average amounts of food, I have two suggestions: (1) buy organic food, and (2) stop wasting food. You will still save $4 per week.

A review paper by Verena Seufert and Navin Ramankutty (2017) of UBC shows that organic crop yields are 19 to 25 percent lower than those in non-organic systems. Let us imagine that mainstream agriculture had evolved differently and that, overall, we produced high-quality food with yields 19 to 25 percent lower than they are today. Could we further visualize a world in which only 15 percent of food was wasted? If that were true, would we aspire to produce 25 percent more food, in order to waste 40 percent?

7

FOOD FOR PEOPLE, FEED FOR LIVESTOCK

Corn flakes, milk so fresh it was warm, sweet strawberries, and a swirl of maple syrup preoccupied us at Grandma's breakfast table. Clinks of spoons and quiet slurps — we didn't want to inspire Grandma's disapproval — receded with the mild announcement, "We'll have chicken for supper tonight." It rather astonished me that Grandma would think to tell us. Her kingdom was the house, where no straw from pant cuffs entered, voices were almost at a whisper, and she served what suited her and we ate it without question. Grampa nodded in agreement to complete the chicken discussion.

The meal finished, Grampa and I stepped outside, our voices rising to fill the barnyard space as we carried the slop to the barn, as a treat for the pigs. I then followed Grampa to the chicken flock grazing on the side of the barn hill where some grain had recently escaped the threshing machine. He surveyed the flock more closely than normal. *What was happening?* He walked toward an older hen. In a smooth sweep he caught her by both legs, stretched her neck on a stump and with his other hand swung an axe I had not previously noticed.

The beheaded hen ran in one direction, then another and another with staggering and drunken steps. Blood speckled green grass like red paint from a mad artist. When I resumed breathing, I sobbed, "Why did you hurt her? How could you?"

My outburst elicited a terse reassurance, "She never felt a thing and she had a good life here," followed by one of his rare explanations: "It was just her nerves made her run."

We resumed our chores and worked in silence for most of the day. I heaved manure until its pungent smell and my sweat combined in an aromatic embrace. We bedded stalls and pens with fresh straw and there was quiet.

That evening in Grandma's kitchen we had chicken for supper. "Can I have more?" I asked, after chewing to the bone the best drumstick I've ever had.

Today I still eat chicken, but only if I know that it's been raised under humane conditions and with a minimum of grain, preferably grain unsuitable for human consumption. Several farmers in my region raise chickens on pasture for at least part of their lives. These birds have room to move about outdoors and are able to consume some forages (e.g., grass, clover) and insects, thus reducing their grain intake. By avoiding crowding in outdoor systems, farmers can reduce or eliminate the use of antibiotics and organic management becomes possible.

Commercially raised broiler chickens are selected for their feed to gain ratio, which is 1.8:1 today (Fry, 2011), a doubling of efficiency since the 1960s (Best, 2011). Poultry scientists are justifiably proud of reducing the required feed from 3.6 kilos to 1.8 kilos to produce 1 kilo of chicken meat. However, if one examines this achievement in terms of increasing the amount of edible food available to humans, it must be concluded that feeding food-grade cereal grains and soybean to chickens is a failure. There would be more edible food available to humans if these crops were not fed to chickens. My Grampa's chickens scratched for insects and grubs behind the barn and scrounged spilled grain. They probably succeeded in eating less human-edible food in feed grain than they provided in eggs and meat.

A goal of sustainable farming and food security is to optimize the availability of human-edible food. For example, a lamb eating grass consumes no human-edible food and all of the formerly human-inedible grass becomes meat and milk. Sheep also produce wool. A dairy cow consuming human-inedible forages and some human-edible grain when she is in early lactation will usually produce more human-edible food in her milk than the combination of calories, protein, and other essential nutrients that would have been available in the human-edible grain alone. On the other hand, if she is fed grain above a certain threshold, she will produce many more litres of milk but not more food value than might have been derived from the extra grain she was eating.

Some of my students have suggested we should use all our arable land to only grow crops for people to eat. This common-sense assertion may need qualification, considering that even very fertile, level fields with stone-free, deep topsoil require forages in some seasons or some years to provide biologically fixed nitrogen, organic matter, and soil cover. Forages also recover nutrients that are not captured by cash crops, and which might otherwise be lost from the field. It should be noted, too, that some farmland has poor fertility, with shallow topsoil and stones on slopes. Here, perennial forages may be the only viable crop. Whether land has very poor or very good soil, agronomists agree that forage cover is necessary. This is needed on a constant basis for conservation of land with poor soil, and at strategic intervals in crop rotations for land with better soil. Crops such as potatoes, carrots, onions, beans, and other vegetables, if grown continuously or even in rotation among these crops alone, will degrade soil quality, regardless of initial soil conditions (Lampkin, 1990).

If we accept that forages are an integral crop on all soils, then we are left with the question of how to deal with the forages. People derive little nutrition from grass and clover. Advocates of grass-fed beef, lamb, and dairy products want these ruminant animals to graze forages or eat stored forages in non-growing seasons (winter and dry seasons). Economists note the obvious added value derived from feeding forages to ruminants.

Soil scientists, for the most part, would be just as happy if the forages were left to grow and wilt as a source of even more organic matter for subsequent human-edible crops. They might note that for the sake of soil health it doesn't matter if forages are digested by earthworms and other soil organisms or by ruminants that offer their manure to the same soil organisms. However, to be practical in commercial food production, there will be no direct economic value from earthworms unless the worms are harvested to use as a bait or to process vermicompost. The forage's residual value to the next crop is usually not included in the calculus of accountants.

Pasture systems, in particular, require little in the way of external inputs and reduce the displacement of nutrients to a minimum. Excreta, deposited directly to the areas where cows are grazing, replaces nutrients in a closed loop (Graves and Martin, 2017). Furthermore, these areas provide cattle and sheep with feed that is clearly not suitable for human food.

Given all of this, it is clear that the practice that makes the most sense is the growing of forages all the time or at intervals to maintain healthy soil. Value can be added to the human-inedible forages by feeding them to ruminants. Have we reached the end of the meat and milk arguments? Obviously not, according to many vegetarians.

Those who advocate vegetarianism for the sake of preventing undue pain and suffering in animals may be correct in their assessment that in the present system of animal husbandry the animals suffer significant distress and pain. However, animals raised under conditions of fresh air, freely available pasture, sufficient supplemental feed, and shelter as required appear not to suffer. In fact, judging by expressions of natural behaviour, they are fulfilled. When these animals are slaughtered on the home farm without being transported to a distant slaughter facility with strange noises, smells, and numerous other stressed beasts, their anxiety is minimized, if not completely avoided. Some farmers are exploring the services of mobile slaughter units for cattle, sheep, and hogs, as well as chickens. Humane and instantaneous slaughter techniques can prevent suffering.

Meat and dairy products are served on the plates of the relatively wealthy. More people in China and India are achieving this status. Global meat production is projected to more than double from 229 million tonnes in 1999–2001 to 465 million tonnes in 2050, while milk output is set to climb from 580 to 1,043 million tones (FAO, 2006).

George Monbiot (2008) reminds us that it's not human population that is the greatest threat to the environment; it's the growing economic activity that we generate, which is exemplified by our growing meat consumption. We eat three times as much meat today as we did in 1980 and about one-third of our grain supply is eaten by farm animals.

Can the trend toward ever more consumption be reversed? There is evidence that it is possible. The Chinese are revisiting the consumption habits in their country. In 1982, Chinese people ate on average thirteen kilos of meat per year, but consumption rapidly climbed to sixty-three kilos per year by 2016; if this trend were to continue, consumption will rise to ninety-three kilos of meat per year by 2030. However, in 2016 the Chinese government set a new goal to go back to thirty kilos of meat per person per year. Since the Chinese are not able to produce sufficient quantities of meat to meet the growing demands of their consumers, they are having to import more. Of course, imported meat is expensive. Reducing the consumption of meat will allow the people to save money. The production of less meat will also — since cattle and other animals emit GHGs — allow the Chinese to reduce GHG emissions by one billion tonnes by 2030. Furthermore, there is urgency to lessen the country's problems with obesity and diabetes (Milman and Leavenworth, 2016).

On June 6, 2017, Michael McCain, president and CEO of Maple Leaf Foods, announced that it is the company's ambition to be the most sustainable protein-packaging company on Earth. He noted that North Americans consume four times more meat than nonindustrial countries, which is unsustainable, while global meat consumption is forecast to rise 80 percent by 2050. It is significant that the prominent Canadian brand associated with meat is now shifting to a broader emphasis on protein.

Willet et al. (2019) recommend that global red meat consumption be cut by 50 percent on average, and of course in regions where high levels of red meat are eaten, the cuts should be more severe. They apply this recommendation to sugar as well, while saying, just like Mom always did, that we should eat more vegetables and more fruit. In fact, they advise an overall increase of at least 100 percent in the consumption of vegetables, fruits, nuts, and legumes (e.g., peas, beans, lentils). A heavy emphasis on plant-based foods with a light stream of animal products could meet caloric needs and shift agriculture from a carbon source to a carbon sink (discussed in chapter 9). Furthermore, Willett et al. (2019) predict that over eleven million deaths per year can be prevented by adopting their "healthy planetary diet."

It is advisable to develop policies to reward farmers for producing animal products with human-inedible feed only. I'm quite sure that if we were to look back in time a hundred years we would find that people did not feed human-edible food to livestock; I think it is safe to assume that a hundred years from now our descendants will understand livestock should not consume human-edible food. We are in an unusual time period, when humans use large swaths of productive agricultural land to grow food-grade crops for livestock consumption. When we stop that, more land will be available for growing human-edible food.

I grant that, because of weather contingencies and other factors, some crops intended for human food will not meet the grade and can therefore be fed to livestock, which will allow such crops to retain some food value. This approach is a return to the original role of livestock in agriculture. With more finessing of food processing, as discussed in chapter 6, and with new technology to process wasted food on plates (the amount of which, of course, should be reduced, as a first goal) there are opportunities to direct more co-products to livestock.

8

OPTIMIZING ENERGY AND NITROGEN USE

In addition to direct sunlight energy, a farm system uses indirect sunlight energy — the stored food energy found in people and draft animals, known as "endosomatic" energy. In modern times, farms (and other enterprises) have come to rely, almost exclusively, on "exosomatic" energy, generated by transforming energy that is external to human and animal bodies. Exosomatic energy is used for tractor fuel, fertilizers, and pesticides, and is embedded in machines, buildings, and other infrastructure. Electricity, derived from the burning of fossil fuels and from nuclear power (and, to a lesser extent in Canada, hydro, wind, solar, and other green sources), while commonly used now to power small motors, lights, and other devices, was used only sparingly before the 1950s.

Farm systems can be designed to produce food units efficiently, per unit of energy input (e.g., kilograms of wheat per litre of fuel). In calculating the energy inputs consumed, it is necessary, of course, to include all the fuel required to operate the tractors and trucks to grow the wheat, and the fuel required to haul necessary inputs to the farm, and to harvest and ship crops from the farm. It's also necessary to include the fuel energy required to manufacture tractors and equipment (pro-rated for their use on the farm's crop), and the fossil fuel required to irrigate the crops, and that required to manufacture, process, distribute, and apply nitrogen (N), phosphorus (P), potassium (K), and other fertilizers, as well as pesticides, herbicides, insecticides, and other such chemicals.

In the last fifty years, North Americans have enjoyed an abundance of cheap fuel and, as a result, our society has become wasteful in its energy use. Energy efficiency has fallen steadily. If we compare the number of calories found in the food produced on our farms to the number of calories used to produce, process, transport, and package this food, we find that agricultural energy efficiency has declined to the point that only one calorie of food output is produced from ten calories of energy input. In other words, our available food has only 10 percent of the energy we put into food systems.

Compare this situation to what is possible when exosomatic energy inputs are limited. I visited Cuba in 1997, where some farms (at the time, at least) relied on energy from oxen and people (endosomatic energy) and, of course, direct sunlight energy. Associated with a university, one farm was monitored meticulously for hours of human and draft animal input. The calculations showed that one hundred calories in food was made available from ten calories of energy input. This Cuban farm was one hundred times more energy efficient than a typical U.S. farm.

There are many explanations for this massive discrepancy in energy efficiency. The very significant amount of exosomatic energy inputs derived from the artificial fertilizers widely used in North American agriculture is one of them. Given that nitrogen fertilizer is very effective in boosting crop yields, it has been applied in increasing amounts to drive more production from each acre of land.

In October 1908, Fritz Haber filed his patent on the "synthesis of ammonia from its elements." This achievement led to his 1918 Nobel Prize in chemistry. His colleague Carl Bosch scaled up the Haber-Bosch process to manufacture large quantities of nitrogen fertilizer. The implications of Haber's relentless tinkering in a lab in Germany, over a century ago, have been profound. Since the First World War, agriculturalists have applied the energy-intensive Haber-Bosch process with zeal. In the last century, the curve on a graph showing the exponential growth of nitrogen fertilizer use overlaps closely with a curve showing energy use in agriculture and also with another curve indicating the growth of human populations. What will the impacts be when fossil-fuel use is restricted?

Nitrogen gas molecules, in the form of N_2 (two nitrogen atoms locked together with triple bonds), make up 78 percent of Earth's atmosphere. Haber-Bosch creates the ammonia needed for fertilizer by splitting these molecules apart using a process that requires a high temperature and high pressure of one thousand atmospheres. Then a hydrogen atom is tacked onto each broken bond of the nitrogen atoms to form NH_3, ammonia. For this transformation, fossil-fuel energy is required; natural gas is the source of the hydrogen.

In contrast to industrial nitrogen fixation, the biological nitrogen fixation process uses very little energy to do the same job. Legume plants (e.g., peas, beans, clovers) receive nitrogen from *Rhizobium*, a lowly bacterium, which associates with the plants, and the *Rhizobium* receive carbohydrates from the legume plants. This trade deal, or symbiosis, is ours to exploit and an agricultural example of civil exchange.

Along with the energy costs, there are other, external costs associated with the industrial manufacturing of nitrogen, costs that are carried by society: nitrous oxide emissions, nitrate pollution in drinking water, and stratospheric ozone depletion. Air, soil, and water pollution, and increased GHGs and, thus, an exacerbation of climate change are all associated with the heavy use of nitrogen fertilizer. Will we be able to feed the world without synthetic nitrogen? Smil (2000) argues that to do so would demand a decrease in human population of between two and three billion.

Fellow agronomists I've talked to agree that feeding 7.6 billion people without nitrogen fertilizer seems impossible. However, Crews and Peoples (2004) suggest that rather than placing our bets on energy-intensive synthetic fertilizer nitrogen, we should rely instead on biological nitrogen fixation with legumes and *Rhizobia*. They document additional savings that could be had if other changes in behaviour were made along with replacing manufactured nitrogen with that produced naturally; such changes would include reducing meat consumption, especially that derived from animals raised in feed lots, and eliminating waste of food. Adopting these changes would go a long way toward creating a more energy-efficient food supply. It is not yet clear what further gains might be achieved by making more widespread other green practices, such as recycling nutrients (including, with safeguards, human sewage), developing urban gardens (recall the Victory Gardens of the Second World War), and farming available productive land near cities.

The increasing use of nitrogen fertilizer following the Second World War produced what is known as the Green Revolution in the middle decades of the twentieth century. The success of this transformation still resonates in agricultural circles. Crop yields and overall food supplies increased during this period. It succeeded because cereal crop plants were bred to take advantage of extra applied nitrogen. Where previously extra nitrogen lengthened and weakened stems of wheat, barley, and other cereal crops, causing them to fall over (or lodge, in the parlance of agronomists), the new strains apportioned more nitrogen to the grain, instead. This improved grain yields and protein content. Crop plants were also bred not only to withstand tighter spacing, but also to grow shorter stems. The result was sturdier plants, even less likely to lodge.

This period also saw the development and use of fungicides to combat diseases that prosper under high densities and lush growth. Likewise, new herbicides took out weeds encouraged by the higher soil nitrogen levels. These military tactics led to spectacular success.

In northwest Europe, relatively high nitrogen fertilizer applications are typical, and as a result conventional farms enjoy high yields, while organic farms yield only 73 percent of their conventional counterparts (de Ponti, Rijk, and Ittersum, 2012). In North America, organic farms produce about 84 percent of the yields of conventional farms, and globally, organic farms have yields at 80 percent of conventional farms. One crop, soybean (a legume that cuts a deal with *Rhizobia* to fix nitrogen), has organic yields that are 92 percent of conventional soybean, whereas organic potatoes, which tend to rely on high nitrogen applications, difficult to achieve with compost or other organic amendments, deliver 70 percent of conventional potato yields (de Ponti, Rijk, and Ittersum, 2012).

What will a retreat from using manufactured nitrogen mean? Vaclav Smil, at the University of Manitoba, argues that 40 percent of people, in 2000, depended on food grown using nitrogen fertilizer, and a more recent estimate by Erisman and others, published in *Nature* in October 2008, is that 48 percent, almost half of humanity, depend on nitrogen fertilizer for their food supply.

Today, some estimate that one-third of the energy consumed in agriculture goes to manufacture nitrogen fertilizer; according to Woods et al. (2010), the nitrogen fertilizer slice of the agricultural energy pie is now at least 50 percent. These numbers refer only to the production of nitrogen fertilizer used in the growing of food crops. Even if human populations do not grow, these numbers are expected to grow, as we are also using nitrogen fertilizer to grow biofuel and biomass crops. Thus, the demand for nitrogen fertilizer is expected to continue expanding, negating the reductions in fertilizer use that might have been achieved from improved efficiencies.

What is the alternative? As mentioned, organic farming is a reliable way to provide the food necessary for human survival while avoiding all of the negative byproducts of yet more nitrogen fertilizer. Organic farms use about half the energy of non-organic farms, mostly because nitrogen fertilizer is not used on organic farms, as noted by Laura Drinkwater and others in their 1998 paper, "Legume-Based Cropping Systems Have Reduced Carbon and Nitrogen Losses," published in the prestigious journal *Nature*.

Although organic farming does require much less energy input, it is criticized for using more land to produce the same total yield. This issue is addressed later in this book. What can be said now, though, is that in addition to using less energy, organic farming conserves soil, water, above- and below-ground biodiversity, and even maintains and restores multifunctional landscapes (Lynch, MacRae, and Martin, 2011). It is also possible for non-organic operations to dramatically reduce nitrogen fertilizer use.

As a result of this reduced reliance on energy input, organic farming outperforms non-organic farming with respect to whole-farm energy use and energy efficiency, especially on a per-hectare basis. Organic farms are also more energy-efficient on a per-farm-product basis, but the advantage is less pronounced because product outputs in non-organic farming are higher per hectare (Lynch, MacRae, and Martin, 2011).

This is obviously good news, but some argue that the energy-efficiency benefits of organic farming may not be sufficient to meet the challenges faced by society:

> While efficiency improvements (per product) sustain food production, they may not in themselves be sufficient. Eventually, the product of excess population, consumption, and waste could exceed global carrying capacity, even if food production becomes more efficient with less energy use per kg food product. For intensity measurements, higher rates of production improve efficiency. The cautionary proviso to the argument that

> more efficient production will address energy
> use and carbon and global warming potential
> impacts is that if the total human impact is so
> large that we exceed carrying capacity, then
> increased efficiency will not be enough to
> avoid system collapse and may, in fact, drive
> us closer to the line. Units of production
> have an upper limit and system resilience
> depends on the continuation of regenera-
> tive inputs and sustainable consumption.
> (Lynch, MacRae, and Martin, 2011)

The increase in fuel efficiency in cars provides a useful comparison. Such measurements of efficiency are calculated using
the number of litres of fuel required for one hundred kilometres
of travel. A reduction in fuel consumption from ten litres of fuel
per hundred kilometres to eight litres of fuel per one hundred
kilometres results in a 20 percent improvement, something we
can cheer. But if this improvement in fuel efficiency is accompanied by a 20 percent increase in the total number of kilometres travelled by all cars, there is no net benefit. Unfortunately,
that is the situation facing the world today with respect to fertilizer consumption.

Hirel et al. (2007) point out that a doubling of global crop
yields over four decades was accompanied by a 700 percent increase in global nitrogen fertilizer use during the same period.
That's a lot of firepower for a yield gain that might have been
accomplished with less environmental impact. Recall that organic crop yields, grown without synthetic nitrogen fertilizer,
are equal to about 80 percent of conventional yields. Organic

farmers and researchers, with their precautionary approach to synthetic fertilizer and pesticides, have chosen to develop efficiencies differently.

Hirel et al. (2007) explain the potential for selecting genotypes that can perform well under low nitrogen conditions.

> Obtaining a satisfactory minimum yield under low N fertilization conditions is therefore one of the most difficult challenges for maize breeders. Instead of developing blind breeding strategies, as was carried out in the past, further research needs to be performed to explain, for example, why certain maize varieties originating from local populations have a better capacity to absorb and utilize N under low N fertilization conditions ... whereas others do not.... This will allow the identification of the morphological (root traits in particular), physiological, and molecular traits that are associated with adaptation to N-depleted soils.

The need to implement such strategies is becoming greater and greater. Steffen et al. (2015) argue that we have clearly crossed the planetary boundary pertaining to excess biochemical flows in our ecosystems; this is particularly true in the case of nitrogen and phosphorus. The planetary limit for additional nitrogen is estimated to be about sixty-two megatonnes per year; currently, however, human activity is resulting in the addition of 150 megatonnes of nitrogen per year. Much of the new reactive nitrogen comes from our relatively recent (in Earth time) adoption of nitrogen fertilizer.

Muller et al. (2017) determined that if global agriculture were 80 percent organic production, then the agricultural nitrogen surplus leaking into the environment every year could be stopped. They also elegantly show that a scenario with 100 percent organic production at a global scale, even with climate change impacts, could provide enough food for the global population in 2050. This hopeful conclusion comes with two key provisos: (1) the amount of food wasted must be reduced by at least 50 percent (discussed in chapter 6); and (2) it is necessary to feed animals with resources that cannot be used for human food consumption (discussed in chapter 7). With 100 percent organic agriculture, though, it could be difficult to access enough nitrogen to maintain production. They suggest this gap could be addressed by improving efficiencies with legumes, capturing more nutrients from organic wastes (possibly even from human waste), and improving nutrient use efficiency in crops.

At this point, general organic standards, which vary slightly from country to country, do not permit the use of human sewage on organic farms. It is understandable that the precautionary principle is applied because the use of human sewage brings with it the risk of the spread of pathogens. Nevertheless, I contend that somehow scientists, farmers, and consumers committed to organic systems will have to come to terms with the fact that we cannot afford to forgo the recycling of the nutrients in sewage. A more deliberate source separation of feces and urine may be necessary, and it is very likely that a composting protocol or anaerobic digestion protocol will be necessary, as will some other process to retain nutrients and prevent problems with pathogens. Of course, the appropriate protocol will have to address pharmaceutical contamination, too. Still, the benefits are too great to ignore.

Humans have been seduced by the potential of nitrogen fertilizer ever since Haber figured out how to artificially produce ammonia in a lab and his buddy Bosch was able to scale it up to industrial capacity. Now, after a century of zealous use of their creation, Steffen et al. (2015) have helped us see the Faustian bargain we accepted. Muller et al. (2017) offer an organic agriculture option, one that could restore balance.

9

WONKY WEATHER AND PROTEAN PRODUCTION

Proteus was the Greek god of the sea and rivers and he had a knack for shape-shifting. He was associated with variability because of the changing nature of the sea and how water changes shape. As we have all come to learn, climate change produces wonky weather, with temperatures and precipitation levels that vary in unexpected ways — sometimes they are too high and sometimes they are too low; sometimes weather that used to be typical of one season now occurs at the wrong time. These variations, especially in water availability, are leading to protean agricultural production, which may be high in some years, and unusually low in others. Certainly, there is much less predictability than what was typical previously.

Bill McKibben, who leads the 350 campaign (350.org), emphasizes that 350 parts per million (ppm) CO_2 in Earth's atmosphere is a safe concentration. McKibben notes that for the period humans have been farmers, the last ten thousand years, we've also had a stable atmospheric concentration of 275 ppm

CO_2. In the last two centuries, but mostly in recent decades, we climbed to above four hundred ppm CO_2 and are still climbing about two ppm per year. We appear to now be outside the Goldilocks window of CO_2 concentration.

Human-induced warming reached approximately 1°C above preindustrial levels in 2017, increasing at 0.2°C per decade (Allen et al., 2018). The Intergovernmental Panel on Climate Change (IPCC) scientists place us in the Anthropocene (the name given to the period extending back approximately two hundred and fifty years, when human activity has been the dominant force affecting climate), beyond the relatively stable Holocene period (the name of the period prior to the Anthropocene era, extending back approximately twelve thousand years — since the end of the last ice age), recognizing that human influence is driving much of the change on Earth.

> Under emissions in line with current pledges under the Paris Agreement (known as Nationally Determined Contributions, or NDCs), global warming is expected to surpass 1.5°C above pre-industrial levels, even if these pledges are supplemented with very challenging increases in the scale and ambition of mitigation after 2030 (*high confidence*). This increased action would need to achieve **net zero CO_2 emissions in less than fifteen years** [emphasis mine]. Even if this is achieved, temperatures would only be expected to remain below the 1.5°C threshold if the actual geophysical response ends up being towards the

> low end of the currently estimated uncertainty
> range. (Rogelj et al., 2018)

Given our current pattern, it is highly unlikely that humanity will achieve net zero emissions in less than fifteen years, at least if the behaviour of the United States is any indication of what actions will be taken. In 2007 their highest GHG emissions from fossil-fuel combustion were just over six billion tonnes per year (Rhodium Group, 2019). The recession of 2008 tugged those emissions down and the decline continued until 2017, albeit at lower rates in 2016 and 2017. However, in 2018 GHG emissions in the United States increased about 3.4 percent. We are off track. Instead of sloping down, even gently, toward zero emissions, our path is climbing again.

The news is even worse than not meeting targets to keep below the 1.5°C increase threshold.

> For oceans … [t]emperature means and extremes are … projected to be higher at 2°C compared to 1.5°C in most land regions, with increases being 2–3 times greater than the increase in GMST [global average surface temperature] projected for some regions (*high confidence*). Robust increases in temperature averages and extremes are also projected at 1.5°C compared to present-day values (*high confidence*). (Hoegh-Guldberg et al., 2018)

We are all in this together. This includes all humans alive today, not just those people who do their part to reduce GHG emissions; it also includes the humans yet to arrive and the other living creatures today, and those expected to live on Earth in the future.

Some argue that the impact of efforts of Canadians, never mind the efforts of one individual Canadian, on addressing this issue are negligible. Since Canadian emissions represent less than 2 percent of global GHG emissions, does it matter what we do? It certainly does. Surely, we lose our moral suasion by waiting for others to start. There's nothing like practice to support a theoretical assertion. If we all keep saying "after you," then the seas will rise, and temperatures and precipitation will fluctuate more and more. The hopeful political dynamic is that action will inspire more action.

I was discouraged to read that Mayer Hillman also says individual efforts are worthless because we're still so dependent on the burning of fossil fuels (Barkham, 2018). However, in a pivot toward hope, Hillman acknowledges that "so many aspects of life depend on fossil fuels, except for music and love and education and happiness. These things, which hardly use fossil fuels, are what we must focus on."

Lest we dither because we want to wait for more evidence, it is prudent to acknowledge that the impacts are already here.

> Human-induced global warming has already caused multiple observed changes in the climate system (*high confidence*). Changes include increases in both land and ocean temperatures,

as well as more frequent heatwaves in most land regions (*high confidence*).... Further, there is substantial evidence that human-induced global warming has led to an increase in the frequency, intensity, and/or amount of heavy precipitation events at the global scale (*medium confidence*), as well as an increased risk of drought in the Mediterranean region (*medium confidence*). (Hoegh-Guldberg et al., 2018)

In 1998, for the first time in Canada, as a result of an ice storm, the Insurance Bureau of Canada recorded over $1 billion in claims associated with a natural disaster and extreme weather (IBC, 2018). This record was broken again in 2005, and it was broken again annually in the period from 2009 to 2013. In 2013, there was a record $3.2 billion payout for natural disasters, and then in 2016 the catastrophic loss total climbed to $5 billion. As a young man, I worked in the insurance industry; during that time I learned that insurance company actuaries are confident about their numbers when they calculate risks. If they think climate change is a risk, and they do, then we should listen up.

The International Institute for Sustainable Development released a report (Bak, 2018) to urge companies to calculate and disclose their physical and business risks associated with climate change. Shareholders have a right to know what the long-term risks are and to press for decisions that will protect them in the future. Shareholders are also becoming concerned about the impacts of their investments on society and on Earth Systems.

In Figure 2 of the paper by Steffen et al. (2018) they show a wavy surface with three troughs, the middle trough representing the Stabilized Earth pathway. They note that in epochs prior to the Holocene, as Earth rolled along the troughs through time, Earth could migrate to the left trough of glacial conditions and then back again over the small hump to the middle trough, where Earth settled in the Holocene. The agricultural production we have become accustomed to is a unique feature of the last ten thousand years of the Holocene. Now, at the beginning of the Anthropocene, Earth has migrated to the right trough of increasing average temperatures and CO_2 concentrations above four hundred ppm. This right trough is labelled the Hothouse Earth pathway.

So far, on the Hothouse Earth pathway, Earth is perched on a very shallow and gently sloping position of the trough. Steffen et al. (2018) argue that only marginally higher GHG emissions, along with intrinsic biogeophysical feedbacks, are required to push Earth from our precarious perch and down toward the deep end of the trough, where conditions would require superhuman interventions to cope, much less to escape. There is uncertainty about whether Earth is already heading un- avoidably downward, or is just one more imperceptible excess GHG nudge away from sliding down. Perhaps humans have the grace of enough time to pull back from the GHG emissions that are pushing Earth downhill. Essentially, this is what Mayer Hillman is so pessimistic about. He's concerned that we are be- yond the point of no return.

The hope and challenge for humanity is to recognize where we are in this still shallow, gently sloping Hothouse Earth pathway. We can try to steward Earth back to the middle trough, the Stabilized Earth pathway. "This steward-ship role requires deliberate and sustained action to become an integral, adaptive part of Earth System dynamics, creating feedbacks that keep the system on a Stabilized Earth pathway" (Steffen et al., 2018).

A practical global financial strategy to reduce GHG emissions is to get rid of fossil-fuel subsidies, currently $500 billion to $600 billion per annum, and to do this by 2020, rather than waiting until 2025 (Rockström et al., 2017). Furthermore, even though food production contributes to more than 10 percent of global GHG emissions, and has weakened natural carbon sinks, agriculture could be designed to not only stop adding CO_2 to the atmosphere, but rather it could remove CO_2 from the atmosphere and sequester it. I am confident that farmers will respond to incentives to manage their crops and livestock to have a net C sequestering impact, if we as citizens support our politicians in appropriate policy efforts. Net C sequestration in agriculture is possible.

As global average temperatures increase, scientists such as James Hansen of NASA advise us to keep the increase to less than 2°C. He argues that in order to return to Holocene conditions and to provide our youth and the next generations the wherewithal to cope, we need to stay under a 1.5°C increase. "That is probably necessary if we want to keep shorelines where they are and preserve our coastal cities" (Watts, 2018).

Rockström et al. (2017) propose a policy option for rapid decarbonization, nothing less than a carbon law. This would entail cutting gross anthropogenic CO_2 emissions in half, every decade. Yes, they are suggesting big cuts with probable disruptive impacts to our ways of living and yet, given our knowledge about the risks we could mitigate, surely it is worth some marginal sacrifices now. This really would be short-term pain, for long-term gain.

How can we start changing? The specific climate impact of air travel per passenger kilometre is up to forty-seven times higher than it is for travel by car, while the specific climate impact per passenger kilometre of buses and trains can be two to five times lower than it is when travelling by car (Borken-Kleefeld, Bernsten, and Fuglestvedt, 2010). We could travel less, and if we must move, we could walk or cycle, or, over longer distances, ride a train or bus. Given that my ancestors were horse-and-buggy Mennonites (some relatives still are), it's not hard for me to see that, in comparison, modern people are extremely restless; they could travel much less, and when travelling they could use more environmentally benign modes of transportation.

There are certainly implications for food production. Gaudin et al. (2015) noted that the yield advantages of corn and soybean in complex rotations (discussed in more detail in chapter 11) were more pronounced in years of stress for crop growth, i.e., when there was a drought or when conditions were too cool and wet for optimal growth. As we approach more variability of weather with climate change, it is well worth noting that more complexity and diversity in crop rotations will help farmers to adapt to wonky weather.

Changes in weather and climate may affect the incidence and severity of insect pests, pathogens, and invasive species

(Dukes et al., 2009). Sometimes as Canadians we are a bit smug about climate change, assuming that perhaps it will lengthen our growing seasons, with more heat each day, to boot. Even if this does occur, we will have to cope with more variability and the risk of more pests and pathogens migrating north.

It has also been established that, in drought years, lower-yielding crops take up fewer nutrients. If farmers apply nitrogen fertilizer, expecting a normal season, the result if a drought occurs is less nitrogen uptake and, therefore, increased residual soil nitrogen (Eilers et al., 2010). When the rains do arrive, and they may occur in downpours, much of that residual soil nitrogen will leach into waterways, where we do not want it.

Li et al. (2009) estimated that global risk of drought will double by 2050, and heavy rainfall events will also increase (Gornall et al., 2010), thus increasing erosion risk and leaching potential.

It is very difficult to model the impact of climate change on agriculture because our experience and knowledge base is of the Holocene, and our Anthropocene experience is still elementary. In the scenario of Steffen et al. (2018), with Earth slowly rolling in the shallow and gently sloping trough of the Hothouse Earth pathway, it is tempting to cling to what we have known. However, it is becoming more urgent to peer at the scenarios of where we might be going and then adjust. Over time and space, farmers have demonstrated amazing agility to adapt. This time it will take more than agricultural technology to cope. It really will require GHG emission mitigation efforts on the part of all humanity to contain the yield-limiting impacts.

Should we leave climate change discussions to scientists alone? Clearly, their data and modelling help us realistically see where we are in the trajectory of Earth's story. However, as whole human beings we will benefit by using all our capacities to address climate change.

Pope Francis issued his encyclical letter "*Laudato Si*': On Care for Our Common Home" in 2015. Since then, criticism of it has come from several sources, including politicians, suggesting that the pope should stick to matters in his church and leave climate change and ecological issues to scientists.

Perhaps anticipating the criticism, Pope Francis referred to his inspirational guide, Saint Francis of Assisi, who "helps us to see that an integral ecology calls for openness to categories which transcend the language of mathematics and biology, and take us to the heart of what it is to be human." And with straightforward candour Pope Francis stated, "our common home is falling into serious disrepair."

Pope Francis goes on to state, "Reducing greenhouse gases requires honesty, courage and responsibility, above all on the part of those countries which are more powerful and pollute the most.... International negotiations cannot make significant progress due to positions taken by countries which place their national interests above the global common good." Although he does not refer to Canada, it is safe to argue that we are failing to adequately support politicians who aspire to address climate change.

Pope Francis addressed his Church followers directly. "We believers cannot fail to ask God for a positive outcome to the present discussions, so that future generations will not have to suffer the effects of our ill-advised delays." It's hard to quarrel with this pragmatic, spiritual admonition.

Mark Carney, a Canadian, and currently governor of the Bank of England, has also warned about the increasing financial implications of climate change and advised insurers that they are heavily exposed to climate change risks. Interestingly, there was less pushback against his warning than might have been expected.

In 2015 a court in The Hague ruled that the Dutch government must cut its greenhouse gas emissions by 25 percent by 2020, rather than their original plan of up to only 17 percent in comparison to 1990 levels. The court not only advised but ruled that the government of the Netherlands has an independent legal obligation to its citizens and not only to other states with which it negotiates.

The Dalai Lama, who can be a burr under some political saddles, also agrees with Pope Francis on climate change and has asked his fellow religious leaders to "speak out about current affairs which affect the future of mankind."

I recall a friend telling me years ago she would stop attending a church because the pastor challenged profligate lifestyles. "She provides empathy and spiritual guidance and yet also leaves me feeling so uneasy every time I go to church," she complained. Minor discomfort now and subsequent action can prevent much more discomfort in the future.

Pope Francis does not limit our search for insights to spirituality. "Respect must also be shown for the various cultural riches of different peoples, their art and poetry, their interior life and spirituality." Today our bent toward continuing with a model of economic growth, too much waste, and too much consumption may be partly due to a lack of imagination about how else we might want to live.

Our Indigenous neighbours' stories involve seeing ourselves in the context of seven generations in the past and seven generations in the future. In support, Pope Francis has said, "It is no longer enough … that we should be concerned for future generations. We need to see that what is at stake is our own dignity. Leaving an inhabitable planet to future generations is, first and foremost, up to us. The issue is one which dramatically affects us, for it has to do with the ultimate meaning of our earthly sojourn."

As painful as it is, a steady look at the prospect of future generations not surviving is required. To dodge this contemplation, because it is too difficult, is no longer an option. Realistic ways forward can emerge from the clear-sightedness of integrative knowing and collective knowledge.

Science can only reveal the trends. It will take many individuals making personal decisions to reduce GHGs of carbon dioxide, methane, and nitrous oxide to reverse trends. Having made personal decisions, we can work with others in our communities to reduce GHG emissions further and to vote practically by selectively buying services and products.

Canada's federal government and its provincial governments wait for us to demonstrate political backing to address climate change. Politicians need to hear that we will support them if they take political risks to develop policy for our broader society to reduce GHGs. Our federal government has put a low price on carbon of $10 per tonne, which will rise $10 per tonne each year, until 2022. Even though the Parliamentary Budget Office has confirmed that this carbon tax is revenue-neutral, because the funds are returned to Canadians, five premiers are objecting to it and claiming it is a tax grab. Regardless, the tepid target of our current and previous federal governments is to reduce GHG emissions by only 30 percent by 2030, contrasted with 2005 emissions. In a clarion call to wrestle with reality, the town of Halton Hills, Ontario, recently set a goal of net zero emissions in their municipality by 2030. They are planning for retrofitting buildings and shifting to electric cars and will have annual reviews to track progress. Political leadership is possible.

International agreements tend to follow awareness and commitments of leading nations. As discouraging as it is to see tentative, inadequate global agreements to address climate change, it is also prudent to get going as individuals and communities. Many already have.

The longer we pretend climate change is not occurring and the longer we postpone our attempts to mitigate or lessen the trend toward extreme water levels and temperatures, the more disruptive and expensive our mitigations will have to be. Similarly, the longer we wait to adapt to wonky weather, the more extreme and expensive our adaptations will have to be.

It is reasonable to fear changes to our way of living, which are set to happen with or without our creative participation. However, the climatic feedback systems of Earth may allow humans to live more fully. Maybe this is an opportunity to wean ourselves from the distractions and unnecessary treats we indulge ourselves with and to, instead, use our intellectual, emotional, and spiritual capacities to understand and nurture what we really need. Perhaps climate change is a grand wake-up call for us to rise up to our authentic human potential.

10

THE FOUNDATION OF
BUILDING SOIL FOR FARMING

The checkerboard of crops on our home farm in Wellington County attested to an annual game plan to optimize soil, crop, and animal health. In the early 1960s, after Grampa died, my father went to the Ontario Agricultural College to check how our approach might be improved.

"Well, let's see," a crop specialist intoned. "You've got to be efficient with the investment in your land, equipment, and buildings. The less turning you have to do in small fields, the better, and if you get set up to grow lots of corn and store it in proper silos, you should be more efficient. If you can grow enough of it, you get what we call economy of scale, and that's not to be sneezed at, no siree. Can save a man a pile of money and grief, to boot." He handed Dad fact sheets with Bible-like columns and diagrams for sound managers.

On the thirty-minute ride home, Dad accepted the future was in corn, every year, for the whole farm. Within three years, the farm gained two silos, a pole barn, cement pads where cattle loafed outside the barn, and manure yards for raising 150 beef cattle. In the fields, fence posts lined up in faithful duty were removed and page wire was rolled up and dumped. Fields between the barn and the train tracks became one, to accommodate faster tillage and long rows of uniform corn.

Fifteen years of continuous corn crops later, I received a letter from Dad, with words sparse as the remaining fence posts in our fields. He asked me to come home and help him put the crop in since he wasn't feeling well.

I rearranged my work schedule, took some holidays, and returned to the family farm for one more spring. The old Cockshutt 40 tractor, bought by our neighbour the year I was born and my field work companion since I was eight, was hooked up to the disks. After greasing all bearings and kicking a few disks I asked Dad where he wanted me to start. "The west side is still a bit damp so why not start on the east side?"

"No problem," I replied, not realizing there was indeed a problem until Dad cleared his throat while looking at the clump of clay he was methodically breaking up with his boot.

"You'll have to work the east side in two fields now." I could barely hear over the sputtering idle of the old 40.

I was about to ask why, paused, and we both stewed in embarrassment. His voice was almost inaudible and I may or may not have heard him say, "Your grandfather was right." Dad took a deep breath, looked me in the eye and, with a sigh of what's done is done, said, "The small gully from the rock pile to the gate on the fence line just kept getting bigger, each year. Tractors can't get through there anymore, so you'll have to work up the back part as a separate field."

We both knew that wasn't the only gully in our mono-cropped corn field. Our eye contact was as brief and profound as the new scars on our farm after millennia of soil development.

It was another ten years before the farm was sold to Mennonite neighbours. I knew Grampa could rest easier then, knowing that the farm had been returned to a good crop rotation, with alfalfa in some of the checkerboard of fields each year, to heal the wounded soil.

The thin membrane of fertile soil that delineates the productive interface of air, minerals, and water in our biosphere is the foundation of agriculture. To form a 2.5 centimetre (cm) depth of soil (340 tonnes per hectare) from bedrock requires two hundred to a thousand years. This is a renewal rate of 0.3 to 2 tonnes per hectare per year. In the United States, soil erosion averages eighteen tonnes per hectare per year (Pimentel et al., 1987). The gospel according to Martin is, "Keep your soil covered." (Too often society chooses to cover the most productive soils, not with beneficial plants, but with developments. That is a clear violation of the gospel according to Martin. On a clear day, from the observation deck of the CN Tower in downtown Toronto, one can see half of the Class 1 agricultural land in Canada. However, most of it is buried under concrete and asphalt.)

If we don't protect our soil, we speed the process of losing it. Productive soil is alive with soil biota, and this vibrant membrane, this crucial organism of Gaia, deserves the protection of living plants. Forage crops (grasses and associated legumes and herbs) are the most effective soil cover. Their roots hold soil in place and add organic matter to it. They are perennial and will be there when rains pelt fields outside the growing season.

Legume forages facilitate nitrogen additions to soil. Annual crops can also be arranged in crop rotations to keep soil covered when cash crops are not growing.

Reduced tillage and no-tillage techniques help to maintain soil integrity. However, until recently, no-tillage techniques also necessitated the use of herbicides. In no-tillage management systems, since the weeds are not being killed by tillage, they are usually destroyed by herbicides. But organic farmers, often accused of releasing too much carbon from soil by excess tillage, have also developed a no-tillage system. A cover crop of rye or vetch or both, for example, is planted in the fall. The next spring a roller crimper (see chapter 4) on the front of a tractor is used to push over the tough winter-surviving cover crop and break up its stems, while a no-till planter on the rear of the tractor can be used to plant soybean. The matted remains of the cover crop help to control weeds and gradually release nutrients to the newly developing soybean crop.

No-tillage systems are poorly suited to incorporating or mixing manure and composts into the soil, however. The transformation and availability of nitrogen and other nutrients for crop uptake is most efficient when manure or compost are thoroughly mixed with the soil. If this is not done, nitrogen is lost as ammonia gas, a detriment to air quality and a loss to the soil-crop system. Generally, organic farmers and others who use forages, manure, and/or composts improve the soil carbon content with some tillage to incorporate it. Teasdale, Coffman, and Mangum, (2007) demonstrated that an organic system with some tillage to incorporate cover crops maintained higher levels of soil carbon and nitrogen concentration than a non-organic, no-tillage system.

Increasingly, farmers are developing ways to build soil more quickly, rather than waiting for natural development from bedrock. Management-intensive grazing, cover crops, and crop rotations are some of the tools. It is crucial that the Ontario government "target funding for longer term research projects (> 3 years), recognizing it takes a long time to see changes in soil health" and "work with Indigenous people and learn from their traditional knowledge of the land" (OMAFRA, 2018).

The information farmers trust most is what they learn from other farmers, especially if they can conduct it on their own farms and discuss it in peer-to-peer learning groups (OMAFRA, 2018). The Farmer-Led Research (FLR) (efao.ca/farmer-led-research/) symposium of the Ecological Farmers Association of Ontario (EFAO) fostered farmer-to-farmer exchanges in early December 2018, prior to the fifth annual EFAO conference in London.

One of the goals of the Practical Farmers of Iowa (PFI) is to create a "culture of curiosity." Both the FLR and PFI programs stimulate curiosity and, even more importantly, make research happen. Ideas sprout, develop into shoots of research, and some mature into improved practices within two or three field seasons. The discarded shoots help busy farmers know what to stop doing.

As an around-the-clock researcher, I was thrilled to witness the energetic interactions during poster presentations of farmer researchers, and then to later listen to numerous hypotheses suggested for testing in 2019 and beyond. In less than three years since our first FLR advisory board meeting, the program is hopping.

As humanity approaches increasing climatic variability, precarious losses of species, and excess biogeochemical flows of nitrogen and phosphorus, FLR can also represent FL Resilience, FL Regeneration, and FL Restoration. Farmers in the FLR program are experimenting and practising for the future.

When I hear a big hairy audacious goal (BHAG) — to use the term coined by James Collins and Jerry Porras for a strategic business statement as dramatic and far-reaching as a vision statement — I expect drum rolls and trumpets; or, if it's really big, tubas. There was not even a piccolo adagio when Abe Collins, a Vermont educator and consultant, shared his passion for topsoil formation and grazing at the 2014 Ecological Farmers Association of Ontario Conference. Nevertheless, the audience was all ears. His BHAG? He expects a certain community, near Lake Champlain, to blanket their watershed in deep topsoil, in a decade.

Abe isn't wild eyed, unusually dressed, or a mesmerizing speaker. His stance is solid as he shows slides of cattle, machines, crops, and soil while sharing his observations about practices on his farm. Like many farmers, he notices details of changes over time. He has seen soil improve and other farmers want to know what his practices are.

One of the startling questions in his presentation was, "Are you happy with farming six inches deep?" Not waiting for a response he said, "Poor farmers grow crops, but good farmers grow soil."

With astute management of keyline plowing (a system of plowing along the contour of a field to reduce compaction and facilitate water infiltration) and management-intensive grazing, Collins's farm "grew" topsoil to a depth of forty-six centimetres, a result that contrasted significantly with an adjacent, set-aside area that had only thirteen centimetres. He claims a subsoiler can buy decades on compacted soil by ripping deep, narrow slots — as moisture seeps deeper, soil microbes go to work, and grass roots explore deeper soil volumes.

Collins considers whole watersheds rather than single farms. He explained that it is cheaper for New York City to pay for preventative water management programs in the Catskills than to pay direct costs of curing polluted and variable water flows. "Topsoil cleans water. Therefore, let's grow more topsoil," urges Collins.

A regional watershed approach could provide social, ecological, and economic benefits. The impact of alternative agriculture is diluted when uniquely managed farms are "islands" among large areas of farms without commitment to such management.

I can imagine creative land use planners of the future designing policy to incentivize organic farmers to congregate on a watershed. There is a unique opportunity to assess an organic watershed on the land expropriated nearly fifty years ago by the federal government for an airport near Pickering, east of Toronto. The airport has never been built, but the land could be preferentially leased to organic farmers and would provide researchers an opportunity to test the efficacy of an organic watershed. To fully optimize the benefits of organic farming, it makes sense to distinguish an organic watershed where all or even a majority of farmers agree to become organically certified (Lynch, Sumner, and Martin, 2014). This would decrease potential contamination by pesticides, and soil and water bodies could be tested. There would also be less risk of transgenic pollen from neighbouring farms. By concentrating expertise, materials, and services required by organic farmers, the synergies of peer mentoring and social support could be realized. It would also create watershed product branding and clean tourism options.

As an excellent grazier, Collins manages his cattle to graze at the right time of grass growth, in exact amounts, with plenty of forage residue to feed the soil. Details of his excellent practices tumble from his mouth, which never seems fast enough for his mind. Regardless, he decries sticking with any one best management practice (BMP) as a primitive relic. "Monitor the outcomes," he urges, "in order to learn faster." These are not the words of a hokey cowboy.

Abe is convinced we can all do better than established BMPs with a real-time dashboard on each farm. Just as some dairy farmers with voluntary milking systems can view monitors with individual cow milking times, milk yield, and health status, he imagines soil-growing farmers regularly checking real-time environmental feedback to land management, with a sensed landscape, to measure soil organic carbon, soil aggregate stability, soil moisture content, other soil characteristics, and weather.

If precipitation can infiltrate into soil with minimal runoff and emerge in creeks as clean water, then soil is well managed, according to Collins. How would sensors on devices such as infiltrometers and penetrometers (to measure compaction) work automatically, on an ongoing basis, at a reasonable cost? That's a challenge for instrument technologists and his computer and big-data colleagues. The synergy of healthy collaboration is to engage people with varying perspectives and skills. Engage them he does.

The social implication is that farmers will be empowered to make local decisions to grow soil, improve water quality, and adapt to the variability of climate change with management that is responsive to what happens, as it happens. Is this what farmers want? It could be their opportunity to sustain soil and crop systems and reverse trends that are keeping them up at night.

Abe told a story about an old man in Australia with considerable business success who told him, "The biggest accomplishment of my life was to build soil with a keyline plow." Many farmers, especially those who have walked and worried on land they have lived on since their birth, know their land has value beyond the calculations of any realtor. Some have heard stories from parents and grandparents about ancestors who also formed and were formed by the same landscape, and they want to do right for their land and their descendants.

Will Abe Collins succeed in his BHAG? I don't know. If not, there will still be improved soil on some farms. If he does, let the tubas play!

Several years ago, I heard Ken Dryden, one of my hockey heroes, interviewed on CBC radio. He caught me by surprise when he said, "Where there is a way, there is a will. Give players a chance to do it right, and they will." He was talking about reducing the risk of concussions. I ran for a pen and a scrap of paper to write it down because I was thinking about farmers and how many of them want to reduce the risk of declining soil health.

Between 2002 and 2016, average soil organic matter (SOM) on Ontario farms declined from about 4.3 percent to below 4.1 percent. The data were compiled by Chris Brown, with the Ontario Ministry of Agriculture, Food and Rural Affairs (OMAFRA), based on twelve thousand to twenty-three thousand annual samples from the SGS Agri-Food Labs.

It was concerning to see, in the same report, that Lambton County (in southwestern Ontario) had an average SOM level of 7.14 percent in 1957, whereas the average level over the last fifteen years was 4.16 percent. That's a drop of three percentage points in about half a century — speeding downhill, in soil time.

Our home farm was in Wellington County, on the border with Waterloo County where I grew up. I took it personally when Brown reported that the average SOM level in Waterloo-Wellington was above 5 percent in 2002, and by 2016 had dipped to less than 4 percent, below the provincial average.

I appreciate that some farmers are doing an excellent job of arresting SOM decline, and in fact are on the long, slow, upward climb. Nevertheless, according to Agriculture and Agri-Food Canada data presented to the Ontario Soil Health Working Group, SOM levels are now decreasing on 82 percent of Ontario farmland.

My farmer-researcher colleague, Woody Van Arkel, a committed cover cropper, notes that it is much tougher to increase SOM than to lose it, so at the very least we should manage crops in order to stop losses. SOM undergirds productive capacity, especially in bad weather years.

Here's another disturbing number: 54 percent of Ontario farmland currently has an erosion risk that is too high (OMAFRA, 2018). As noted earlier, the soil renewal rate ranges from 0.3 to 2 tonnes per hectare per year (Pimentel et al., 1987), while soil is disappearing faster than that on many fields.

Over the last twenty-eight years, my long-suffering students have had to memorize the aforementioned gospel according to Martin: "Keep your soil covered." Today, across Ontario, only 20 percent of cropland has high to very high cover (i.e., more than three hundred days covered) (OMAFRA, 2018). When bare ground is pounded by rain, it erodes and loses SOM.

If determined, we could ensure that within five years at least 50 percent of all fields in Ontario are covered in the vulnerable-to-erosion, non-cropping season of November to April, and within ten years, 100 percent. Fields could be monitored with satellites, aerial sensors, or both. So far, the political will is lacking among farm organizations and OMAFRA to set such goals. Nevertheless, the percentage of farmers using cover crops doubled (from 12 percent to 25 percent) between 2011 and 2016 (OMAFRA, 2018), although not necessarily during the high erosion risk period of November to April.

BMPs are important, but it is crucial to employ them in appropriate combinations for each specific field, in a persistent manner. It is not enough to promote such practices if they are adopted only when it suits, or in response to temporary incentives for one BMP at a time.

We need the ongoing attention of all operators. Part of the problem is that landowners increasingly rent their land to operators or consolidators of large land bases, who spread costs over more acres, with just two or three crops, and then accept the collateral damage of declining SOM levels.

The Agricultural Soil Health and Conservation Working Group set a farm scale measure of success as being at least a "good" rating of SOM, based on soil texture: sandy soils at 2.5 percent, sandy loams at 3.5 percent, loam soils at 4 percent, and clay loams and clay soils at 4.5 percent (OMAFRA, 2018). It makes sense that SOM levels should be expected to be higher on clay loam or clay soils than on sandy soils.

As a member of this working group, I proposed that we go further with policy to ensure we meet the outcome of at least a "good" rating for SOM. I had to accept that the majority of my colleagues did not support my suggestion. I suggested that in order to stop the decline of SOM, and to begin recovering past losses, it is time to link SOM levels to farm property taxes. Farmers now pay a preferred property tax rate because they are farming. Fair enough, but to be more fair, those who have good or very good levels of SOM, or who are increasing their SOM levels, should pay even less property tax. They are investing in the foundation of food production.

On the other hand, landowners with SOM levels that are poor or declining should reasonably pay more property tax. If that were the case, they would make sure their rental agreements included clauses about good soil management, first to prevent SOM losses, and then to improve them.

I understand that municipalities should not be hit with revenue reductions. The provincial government can underwrite a property tax program, adjusted to SOM levels. All citizens, now and in the future, deserve a system that will ensure proper soil management and increasing SOM levels. Our civil servants and government can make it happen if they put their minds to it.

To accomplish this, it would be necessary to measure SOM in every field, every five years, with a consistent scientific protocol. This database, and some math, will make property tax adjustments possible. Let's design for the outcome of SOM levels that we need. The old adage is to measure what we treasure.

The Senate Standing Committee on Agriculture and Forestry (2018) recommended that federal government departments "undertake and/or support research that will help to establish baseline levels of soil organic carbon [directly correlated to SOM] to support the development of offset protocols for carbon sequestration across Canada."

We want to sequester carbon in soil to build SOM, and we also want to reduce its concentration in air. Regenerative farming can deal with both, by (1) pulling carbon dioxide out of the air, and (2) building SOM by sequestering carbon in the soil.

At the Ecological Farmers Association Conference in December 2018, I was struck by the innovation of Elizabeth and Paul Kaiser of Singing Frogs Farm, in Sebastopol, California (singingfrogsfarm.com). Their SOM is now 8.5 percent in their no-till, no-spray, highly diverse vegetable farm. Their five principles are: (1) disturb soil as little as possible, (2) include living plants as often as possible, (3) foster as much plant diversity as possible (including perennial hedgerows of bushes, vines, and trees), (4) keep the soil covered (big smiles from me as they explained this), and (5) incorporate animals (they made multiple references to birds, snakes, bees, and imported organic horse manure).

At the end of their presentation, they disclosed that their gross income is $100,000 per acre, whereby 70 percent of revenue goes to employees with ratios of 1.5 to 2 full-time-equivalent employees per acre. Paul noted that in spite of recent fires and floods (part of their farm is low lying) they have resilience, largely attributed to high SOM levels. His parting shot was that 70 percent of the world's food is produced on farms that are two hectares or less.

Farmers are clever and adaptable. With independent thinking, research, and peer support programs, they will figure out how to improve SOM levels and reduce their taxes. Like Ken Dryden's hockey players, farmers, given a chance, will do it right. "Where there is a way, there is a will."

11

RECOVERING DIVERSITY

The universe is a wonder, perhaps too grand to contemplate, and it is our home — a home that we are truly blessed to have. After the great flaring forth of the universe, as Thomas Berry (1990) so aptly phrased it, 13.5 billion years ago, there occurred a great many grand cosmic events. Let's say the one-year story of Earth begins, about 4.5 billion years ago, on January 1, when Earth formed. On February 18, 3.9 billion years ago, photosynthetic bacteria appeared.

It took until June 11, or 2.5 billion years ago, for oxygen and ozone to become apparent, and it was not until some six hundred million years ago (November 12) that multicellular organisms and animals began to grace our planet. A short while later, 440 million years ago (November 25), plants emerged from the sea.

Although often considered to be from the distant past, dinosaurs arrived relatively recently in Earth's story, 145 million years ago (December 19); they then disappeared in an extinction event, 67 million years ago (December 25 at 10:30 a.m.).

Following the dark period after the dinosaurs' demise, the Cenozoic era began — sixty-five million years ago, on December 25 at 5:30 p.m. The amazing diversity of life this era spawned appeared at a time when many celebrate the joy of a new beginning, with a Christmas feast.

Our species of wonderful creative genius, and also, unfortunately, horrifically destructive capacity, first walked on Earth about two hundred thousand years ago (December 31 at 11:37 p.m.). The Holocene, the last ten thousand years, when conditions have been unusually benign for agriculture, started a mere seventy seconds before the present in the one-year story of Earth. The last one hundred years, when agriculture and human population have grown dramatically, are only 0.7 seconds of the story: barely enough time to blink.

Several philosophers and theologians, including Thomas Berry, have warned that, just like Dorothy in *The Wizard of Oz*, we are not in Kansas (the Holocene) anymore. We have crossed into a new epoch, the Anthropocene. "It's the first time in Earth's history that a single species — *Homo sapiens* — has had such a powerful impact on the planet" (Grooten and Almond, 2018). Steffen et al. (2018) agree that we are in new adaptive circumstances.

> The formalization of the Anthropocene as a new geological epoch is being considered by the stratigraphic community, but regardless of the outcome of that process, it is becoming apparent that Anthropocene conditions transgress Holocene conditions in several respects. The knowledge that human activity now rivals

geological forces in influencing the trajectory of the Earth System has important implications for both Earth System science and societal decision making.

The question is, how, with all of our knowledge, including our knowledge of the current state of Earth, will we choose to treat the grand gift of our incredible inheritance? We could choose, because of neglect or hubris, to continue to be immersed in daily pursuits of acquisition to extract yet more from Earth, with a sense of entitlement.

Alternatively, as evolved and awakened creatures, we can humbly pursue a higher purpose. That would include addressing climate change and reducing our impact on Earth, while alleviating poverty. The ending of the first year of Earth's story necessarily hails the start of a new year. As humans face this, with awareness of who we are on Earth, we have a call for participatory authorship as the story unfolds (Teilhard de Chardin, 1972). Teilhard, a Jesuit priest and paleontologist, imagined we would humbly and reverentially evolve to increased complexity and increased interconnectedness and eventually gain an ultimate point of union with God. If he were still alive, I'm guessing he would mourn our regression to less complex and less interconnected relationships with the natural world.

E.O. Wilson, professor of biology at Harvard University, exhorts us in his 2007 book, *The Creation: An Appeal to Save Life on Earth*, to "stop exhausting earth's bounty before we live in total desolation. Why wait until the seas are stripped of their denizens and the lands reduced to barren deserts, with only the ever present bacteria thriving beneath the surface?"

That would be regressing to August 9 in our one-year story of Earth. Rather, Wilson tells us to "preserve nature for its own sake because we love it." The Biodiversity Project conducted polls of Americans in 2002:

> Respect for God's work, respect for nature for its own sake, the need to provide for future generations, the appreciation of the beauty of nature, the need to maintain a balanced healthy life, and the expectation as an American citizen to protect natural resources all were regarded as "extremely important" reasons for protecting the environment by a large percentage of respondents. (Novacek, "Engaging the Public," 2008)

These are crucial times for our Earth. After 4.5 billion years it is not clear that we will have another such "calendar year" ahead of us, nor even a blink. Earth will survive, of course, but will we be part of its future? Will the other creatures that we share the planet with? Thomas Berry (1990) paints the picture of being at a fork in the Anthropocene road. We can continue on the current path of what he labels the "Technozoic," with its human hubris and ecological suffering. Or we can choose the path of the emerging "Ecozoic," with an attitude of reverence and knowing our place within Earth. From a food security perspective, I suggest that we can tip the choice toward the Ecozoic by finding answers to the question, "How will we eat well in our sustainable communities?"

We don't know if we will survive as a human species. We may and we may not. Earth is more likely to survive, regardless of our fate, but it is also seriously at risk. The issue is simply that stark, and that urgent.

We must not only accept the realistic conditions necessary for us to survive, we should, even better, try to authentically embrace our humble place on Earth. If we are to be serious about sustaining communities and moving beyond platitudes (that we may have no intention of addressing, but which we dare not oppose), then we must realistically assess what is required for sustenance. Having made that assessment, we can decide whether to do this, or not. If we do want to achieve resilience, then let's roll up our sleeves and do it.

The abundant biodiversity we were granted at the beginning of the Cenzoic era (dinner on Christmas Day) is rapidly disappearing. The planetary boundary for reactive nitrogen in our biosphere was discussed in chapter 8. This has been exceeded. Steffen et al. (2015) elucidate how we have gone too far beyond another planetary boundary, i.e., extinctions per million species-years (E/MSY). E/MSY should be less than ten, with an aspirational goal of about one. However, E/MSY now is actually between one hundred to one thousand extinctions per million species-years: orders of magnitude above evolutionary background levels.

Assuming that the human species has survived for two hundred thousand years, our extinction would be a small blip on the E/MSY, i.e., about 0.2 E/MSY. It seems we don't understand how vulnerable we are, as we lose other species. The species loss problem is serious, yet, given that measurements are inexact, there is a risk we may tip into irreversible changes before we know the boundary has been crossed.

Furthermore, Steffen et al. (2015) explain that biodiversity supports ecosystem functioning with complex relationships and interactions that are difficult to untangle and document. A Biodiversity Intactness Index (BII), where applied, indicates that ecosystem degradation and loss of ecosystem productivity are evident with measured BII decreases.

Steffen and his colleagues in their 2018 paper draw our attention to the combined impact of climate change and species loss.

> Current extinction rates are at least tens and probably hundreds of times greater than background rates, and are accompanied by distributional and phenological changes that disrupt entire ecosystems both on land and in the sea. The rate of homogenization of biota … has risen sharply since the mid-20th century.… [C]onditions of the mid-Holocene and the Eemian are already inaccessible because CO_2 concentration is currently ~ 400 ppm and rising, and temperature is rising rapidly towards or past the upper bounds of these time periods. (Steffen et al., 2018)

In a specific location in the Luquillo rainforest of Puerto Rico, Lister and Garcia (2018) reported that the overall weight of arthropods had plummeted by ten to sixty times from the 1970s to this decade. Lizards, frogs, and birds that rely on arthropods as a food source also declined, precipitously. Lister and Garcia clearly associate higher forest temperatures and climate change, independent of habitat decline, with this collapsing food web.

Insect biodiversity in the world has been plunging, with estimates that about 50 percent of insect species are rapidly dropping in population and about 33 percent of insect species are close to extinction (Sánchez-Bayo and Wyckhuys, 2019). However, Sánchez-Bayo and Wyckhuys concluded, unlike Lister and Garcia (2018), that the main drivers are habitat change, especially by agricultural displacement of natural habitat and by relying so heavily on monocrops where land is farmed. Sánchez-Bayo and Wyckhuys (2019) state that the next largest driver is synthetic pesticides, followed by synthetic fertilizers. We dare not ignore the impact of insect species loss. "Unless we change our ways of producing food, insects as a whole will go down the path of extinction in a few decades. The repercussions this will have for the planet's ecosystems are catastrophic to say the least, as insects are at the structural and functional base of many of the world's ecosystems."

In the fall of 2018, the World Wildlife Fund released their Living Planet Report (Grooten and Almond 2018), with the shocking news that wildlife populations declined by over 60 percent in just over forty years.

> There cannot be a healthy, happy and prosperous future for people on a planet with a destabilized climate, depleted oceans and rivers, degraded land and empty forests, all stripped of biodiversity, the web of life that sustains us all[;]... for the first time, we can fully grasp how protecting nature is also about protecting

> people. The environmental and human development agendas are rapidly converging.

The World Wildlife Fund (2018) report goes on to link biodiversity loss to agriculture. "Of all the plant, amphibian, reptile, bird and mammal species that have gone extinct since AD 1500, 75% were harmed by overexploitation or agricultural activity or both." As humans, we have become so clumsy at extracting our food from nature that we are destroying other species, often without awareness.

The lack of awareness extends to an ignorance of the ecological impact of cultivating just a few species in order to maximize yields. There are about 350,000 plant species and 195,000 flowering plants, most of which have edible parts useful to humans (FAO, 2019). The Food and Agriculture Organization (FAO) of the United Nations report goes on to explain that only about one hundred plant species are actually used for human food. Remarkably, we restrict ourselves to seventeen species to provide 90 percent of our food.

In 2016, I heard a hopeful talk by Dr. Allen Van Deynze of the African Orphan Crops Consortium. He explained how their goal is to improve resilience and the productivity of 101 traditional African food crops, which are already nutritious (AOCC, 2018). During the question period I revealed some of my ignorance by asking him how the African Orphan Crops Consortium was unique. With a smile he said, "The Bill Gates Foundation endeavors to make a few productive crops more nutritious, while we train African scientists to make numerous native nutritious crops more productive."

To address species loss, it is necessary to consider not only those species impacted by agriculture, but also those that can be directly included as agricultural crops. Resilience, in a time of climate change, excess nitrogen and phosphorus in our biosphere, and species loss, can be partly restored by broadening our food crop species base, with the attendant reinforcement of entomological, pollination, avian, fungal, bacterial, and plant interconnections.

In chapter 1, I referred to Paul Wartman, who did his graduate research with me and my colleague Rene Van Acker, on a forest garden system (FGS). It was difficult to design a study that he could conduct within a two-year timeline for an M.Sc. project and he quite reasonably objected to my pitch of doing a twenty-year graduate project. We agreed to establish apple trees under four treatments: (1) a complex understory of diverse, perennial support plants with compost; (2) the same complex understory without compost; (3) a simple grass understory mixture with compost; and (4) the same grass understory without compost. The complex understory included perennials with multiple functions of nitrogen fixation, nectary sources for pollinators and beneficial insects, reduced weed competition, and prevention of cultivation.

> Diverse perennial plants contribute to ecosystem functions through nutrient accumulation, carbon (C) sequestration, water storage and filtration, production of food (e.g., fruits, nuts, greens, sugars and fodder), medicine and other yields for human use, as well as habitat creation and shelter.... This study was the first to report

> research results in establishing a temperate
> FGS. We conclude that FGSs can benefit ap-
> ple orchards by increasing the growth of apple
> trees. (Wartman Van Acker, and Martin, 2018)

The project was an excellent first step to assess FGSs
and would have required more time to determine differences
between microbial diversity under the two main systems for
bacteria, archaea, fungi, arbuscular mycorrhizal fungi, nutrient
cycling of nitrogen-fixing plants, and soil microbe interactions.
Such research requires long-term planning to include various
graduate students at different stages of the project. It will also
be tricky to find funds because it may not lead to obvious short-
term financial paybacks. Most research requires some money
from industry (to demonstrate its applicability) to leverage
more government funding. Commitments of research funds
beyond a five-year term are very rare.

In the 1980s, after having been out of university to explore
nonacademic ways to live, I returned to academia to conduct
research on growing corn and pole beans together. My super-
visor at Carleton University, John Lambert, had intrigued me
with a presentation of similar research he was conducting in
Belize. My previous inquiries in a Unified Liberal Arts Program
may not have seemed applicable for an M.Sc. in biology and
yet it was precisely because of my training to look closely at

presuppositions that I was able to see that intercropping has a traditional and foundational future role in crop production, in spite of apparent impracticalities. It is only impractical if we allow current production paradigms to limit alternatives.

The objections at the time, most of which persist today, with two or more crops grown simultaneously on the same field, are that (1) there is competition between the crops for light, nutrients and water; (2) it is difficult to control weeds with herbicides in crops with varying susceptibilities; (3) the timing of planting and harvesting are different; and (4) it is tricky enough to set a combine harvester to cleanly harvest one crop over a variable field, let alone additional crops. In traditional systems of human intervention, i.e., those by hand, it was only the competition factor that required optimization. Technology had added constraints to imitating natural systems, mostly because it has been aimed to optimize growth and yield of one monocrop at a time.

Early in my intercropping research and during delightful days of digging in the literature, I found this admonition, which sustained me through the drudgery of separating beans from leaves and from vines, and corn cobs from stalks. "Since human beings have not yet advanced to the point of evolving a totally new and well-adjusted ecosystem, they have to follow closely on nature's heels. This is precisely what mixed cropping does. Although it is not a perfect replication of nature, its environmental rationale is far superior to that of monoculture" (Igbozurike, 1971).

Later in my Ph.D. research to investigate intercrops of corn and soybean, I was able to show that corn-soybean silage had higher protein concentrations than corn silage alone, an important factor when feeding dairy cows. Furthermore, corn-soybean intercrops had a range of cost-effective (accounting for seed costs, fertilizer costs, and crop yields) advantages from $132 per hectare to $261 per hectare, contrasted with growing corn alone (Martin, Voldeng, and Smith, 1990). We also established that European Corn Borer (a persistent pest in corn crops) infestations were lower in corn-soybean intercrops than in monocropped corn (Martin et al., 1989) and that nitrogen fixed by soybean was transferred to intercropped corn as the two crops grew together (Martin, Voldeng, and Smith, 1991).

Land equivalent ratios (LERs) were used to compare the intercrop yield of corn to the monocrop yield of corn (ratio 1) and the intercrop yield of soybean to the monocrop yield of soybean (ratio 2). In our case, on average, ratio 1 was about 0.8 and ratio 2 was about 0.4. Yes, both crops yielded less than they would have in monocrops; however, to appropriately attribute the efficiency of land use, the two ratios were added, and the final LER was 1.2. This means that if a farmer wants both corn (for feed biomass and energy) and soybean (feed protein), then they will gain an efficiency of 20 percent (LER = 1.2) by growing the two crops together on twenty hectares rather than separately on ten hectares for each crop (Martin, Voldeng, and Smith, 1990).

Later, there was more research to find ways to make the corn-soybean intercrop system as suitable as possible for modern farmers (Martin, Astatkie, and Cooper, 1998). Nevertheless, the uptake was minimal. Granted, it does involve more steps and more fiddling. I learned that farmers respond to how much they are paid, and to date there are very few avenues for them to be paid for increasing biodiversity.

As policy options are considered to address the serious biodiversity losses noted above, I want to be clear that my research showed that corn-soybean intercropping is not only possible but profitable. That was before technology developments of steering guidance systems for exact planting and harvesting, organic no-till systems (see chapter 4), and sensors capable of separating bean seeds from corn seeds. If intercropping is deemed to be worthwhile, it can be done.

Now, a few decades later, one of my graduate students, Kyra Lightburn, with a work ethic seldom seen and a determination to match, is applying her considerable intellectual acuity to understanding how pollinators are affected by forage mixtures and grazing patterns. She is investigating forage biomass, floral diversity, and pollinator species and populations on ten independent pairs of organic and non-organic rotationally grazed cattle pastures in southern Ontario. The farms were selected and matched based on climatic and geological similarities. Initial data shows there is increased floral abundance and diversity as well as more forage biomass on the organic farms.

> The biodiversity thriving in grass and pasture-
> land systems is indispensable to the healthy
> growth and functioning of agricultural eco-
> systems and, therefore, necessitates conser-
> vation and enrichment. This research will
> produce important management recommen-
> dations targeting maximum support for wild

> bee populations in these systems. Moreover,
> by improving the knowledge of the resourc-
> es and management strategies that best boost
> specific species populations in their preferred
> habitat-types, the results will be foundational
> to future research and efforts regarding cru-
> cial habitat creation in other agro-ecosystems.
> (Lightburn, Martin, and Raine 2018)

There are numerous benefits to having perennial forage crops, especially red clover and other forage legumes, on the landscape (Gaudin et al., 2013). Forages reduce erosion and compaction and increase soil organic matter, microbial activity, and water holding capacity, to name a few benefits other than those attributed to pollinators.

For all the benefits of forage crops, there is increasing resistance to the growing of them because the foragers are ruminants, cattle and sheep. They emit methane, a greenhouse gas with about thirty times more warming potential than CO_2. However, Stanley et al. (2018) demonstrated that with well-managed grazing, i.e., adaptive multi-paddock (AMP) grazing, GHG emissions could be offset through soil carbon sequestration. Therefore, this type of grazing can be a net carbon sink. They acknowledge that AMP grazing requires twice as much land as feedlot-finished beef, and this implies that less beef will be produced in any given region; however, there is the benefit of net carbon sequestration. We need more carbon in the soil and less in the air (chapter 10). Stanley et al. (2018) show how this can be accomplished. Furthermore, people experience health benefits by eating grass-fed beef, and by eating less meat overall. Half of current beef consumption will meet all our dietary needs.

Regardless, of management options to reduce GHGs or even to achieve net sequestration of C, there is a growing interest in cover crops as soil stabilizers within cash crop systems. I recall Eliot Coleman (fourseasonfarm.com), an organic farmer from Maine, speaking at a conference. He noted that he can feed forages to livestock even if he doesn't have beef cattle or sheep. He can feed earthworms and other soil life with forages.

As a patient reader, you will know by now that the gospel according to Martin is to "keep your soil covered." However, cover crops do more than cover soil and prevent erosion. Sometimes they are also catch crops, catching nutrients, especially nitrogen, which might otherwise be leached into the water table. Break crops are grown between cash crops to break disease cycles, and smother crops will smother weeds. Then there are the floral services they provide for pollinators — birds and insects.

Another wonderful graduate student (I'd be a much poorer man without them), Cameron Ogilvie, went to great lengths one day to convince me we should update our language from "cover crops" to "service crops." He argued that service crops are plants grown in agroecosystems for the ecosystem services they provide, rather than a harvestable product. These services extend beyond soil cover. He's right, and I've since used his terminology. Fortunately, my acceptance of his argument did not dim his enthusiasm to keep making his case and he did a first-rate job of scouring the literature to write a review paper, "Service Crop Management to Maximize Crop Water Supply and Improve Agroecosystem Resilience" (Ogilvie, Deen, and Martin 2019).

> Service crop polycultures—in contrast with monocultures—have the greatest potential to provide the service of agroecosystem resilience, and if properly managed, a grass/legume/tap-root service crop mixture could maximize multifunctionality while also avoiding the set-backs associated with the component species when grown in monoculture.

There are many opportunities to improve biodiversity in agriculture, including permaculture farms, characterized by high species diversity, divided among multiple unique polycultures (Hirschfeld, 2017). Elizabeth and Paul Kaiser of Singing Frogs Farm (chapter 10) not only increased their SOM to 8.5 percent but their farm is singing with biodiversity.

At a conference about two decades ago, I encountered Dennis Avery (heartland.org/about-us/who-we-are/dennis-avery), who explained in his keynote talk that by encouraging farmers to dramatically increase inputs on well-managed farmland, society would benefit by having more land available for Bambis and bunnies, since more natural land would be spared by highly intensive agriculture. As you may surmise from what I've previously written, I did not agree and made the point during the Q&A period that ecological boundaries are not solid walls. The ecological boundary between an intensive farm and a wetland is porous to flows of pesticides, excess nutrients, and eroding soil. Increasingly, the risks of treating soil as a substrate for ever higher rates of inputs (many offered by companies that Avery represents) are becoming more apparent.

It is possible to manage agricultural land to reduce inputs, improve SOM, and increase biodiversity. It is possible to be frugal with how much money leaves the farm for inputs of pesticides, fertilizers, and equipment, and to arrange for higher profits to stay on the farm.

In an experiment that has been ongoing for almost forty years at the Elora Research station associated with the University of Guelph, over the decades of the research, there have been higher corn and soybean yields, enhanced yield stability, and improved SOM when corn and soybean crops were integrated into diverse rotations with forages, rather than being in simple rotations of corn and soybean alone (Gaudin et al., 2015). For example, the complex rotation of corn in year 1, corn in year 2, soybean in year 3, and winter wheat (with red clover frost seeded on snow in the early spring) in year 4, had higher corn and soybean yields, enhanced yield stability, and improved SOM than a monocrop of corn every year or than a simple rotation of corn and soybean in alternate years. In each case, after four years, the rotation was repeated for another four years. Unfortunately, most current rotations in Ontario consist of only corn and soybean.

The striking observation by Gaudin et al. (2015) was that the yield advantages of corn and soybean in complex rotations were even more pronounced in years of stress for crop growth, i.e., when there was a drought, or when conditions were too cool and wet. As we approach more variability of weather, with climate change, it is well worth noting that more complexity and diversity in crop rotations will help farmers to adapt to wonky weather.

"The benefits of organic management for biodiversity of wildlife on farmland are clear, with a typical increase in organism abundance of 40 to 50% across different taxa" (Seufert and Ramankutty, 2017). They also reported that organic agriculture has a stronger effect on biodiversity in arable systems than in grassland systems, as might be expected, given the intense monocropping of two or three crops in arable systems of non-organic agriculture.

Freemark and Kirk (2001) assessed populations of birds on seventy-two field sites in southern Ontario, paired between ten organic and ten conventional farms, for local habitat. Species richness and total abundance were significantly greater on organic than on non-organic farms.

As a possible explanation for results reported by Freemark and Kirk (2001) and others, Girard, Mineau, and Fahrig (2014) determined that the overall nestling food biomass (small invertebrates, necessary for growth and survival of the young of many songbirds) was significantly greater on organic fields than on non-organic fields.

Overall agroecosystem biodiversity can be enhanced by subscribing to organic standards and avoiding the use of synthetic pesticides and fertilizers, and including more diversity of crops and crop rotations, which are usually required to maintain productivity without synthetic inputs.

Biodiversity can be enhanced by agriculture in several ways, and wide-awake farmers are showing us how. Agriculture does not have to have the reputation of contributing to diminishing biodiversity.

12

QUINTESSENCE

In some traditions, ether was considered the fifth of the essential elements — the others being earth, air, fire, and water — that make up the universe. This "quintessence" (the word comes from the Latin for "five") was believed to be the "breath of the gods" and to pervade all things. Following from this, the term *quintessence* has come to be used to describe the purest and most perfect form of a quality. Even if we doubt the existence of a fifth element (as it was formerly conceived), let us suppose that there still exist ideal qualities and that we can aspire to these. What would they be?

Surely, we desire the purest and most perfect form of our relationships. We seek to transcend our egos and live lives of love and selfless service to other people, including enemies. Of course, we are not just members of a human community; we are connected to all and everything that we share our planet with: animals, plants, and even the non-living elements. We are linked among stars and atoms in a relational dance of reverence, in an awestruck reverie at the wonder of it all and our place in it.

Although it has been shown that a number of animal species display significant intelligence and other higher-order faculties, it seems that after 4.5 billion years of Earth's evolution, humans alone are capable of reflecting on the planet and its myriad other beings, past, present, and future. Surely some reverence is in order.

Thomas Berry, Brian Swimme, Joanna Macy, and others have elucidated a spiritual approach to ecology. In a sense, they borrowed and adapted this from Indigenous Peoples, who routinely integrated spirituality and life-support systems. Obliged to survive worsening times, we may yet again learn reverence and awe for the cosmos and a healthy respect for Gaia. We in the West, like our forebears, may regain thankfulness for our daily bread.

In 1973 Arne Næss introduced the concept of "deep ecology" (Drengson, 2005). The philosophy of deep ecology assumes that nature has inherent value and is not solely of use to humans. Næss believed that humankind sees itself as the pinnacle of evolution only because humans do the ranking. He wondered how it was that other organisms have been able to eventually find a state of equilibrium with their respective biospheres, while we, in our raiding arrogance, tend to overwhelm and destroy the environment in which we live. Deep ecology advocates a paradigm shift, the adoption of a way of life in harmony with nature rather than the one that is our present approach, in which we claim mastery over it.

In 1997, I spent a sabbatical in Cuba. I was struck by the opportunity of Cubans who had three essential ingredients that could help them to successfully adopt and implement deep ecological principles: (1) their isolation from much of the world markets has made it necessary for them to live with few fossil fuels, pesticides, and other industrial inputs; (2) they are well-educated about holistic science, ecosystems, and producing within biological constraints; and (3) they have a collective memory of a recent historical precedent for implementing progressive policies that resulted in a quantum leap of life quality for most of the population (Martin, 2000). Since my visit, Cubans have become somewhat more prosperous and I worry that their deep ecology potential has lessened.

I'm often struck by our refusal to deal with the real issues confronting us, issues requiring significant changes in how we live. Ecological realities and Mother Earth's corrective measures may involve discomfort, pain, and angst. Why not use Joanna Macy's philosophy to acknowledge the despair that we genuinely feel and to help us see clearly and keep going regardless?

We already have insights from wisdom traditions to balance despair, and hope can emerge from despair. Granted, talk of despair turns people off. But that is no reason to de-emphasize it or to play down our bad habits, which harm nature. Gaia will make the necessary ecological shifts, with or without our co-operation. They could have profound implications for human well-being. The job ahead will require tough choices, which I doubt we can dodge. Nevertheless, we can't afford the luxury of sinking into cynicism. Restoration will involve love, and hearts open to possibilities.

This is not a matter of crying "Wolf!" where no danger exists. It seems to me that keeping silent for fear of offending is not an option. When the ecological pennies drop — as they assuredly will — those we've shielded from the truth could rightfully chide us for not raising the alarm. When the house is on fire, we don't stand on ceremony.

Michael Novacek ("It Happened," 2008), a paleontologist, senior vice-president and provost of the American Museum of Natural History, was alarmingly frank. "We may not be able to determine the cause of past extinctions, but this time we know the cause indisputably; we are our own asteroids." He doesn't shirk from accusations of doom-saying, from those who argue that a bit more economic growth and human ingenuity will see us through. He flatly states that "The sixth extinction event is under way." And he is not alone. Virtually all climatologists and ecologists in the Intergovernmental Panel on Climate Change and in other organizations agree we have a worsening problem.

Surely, if the news is so negative, we must address it. To look away because the prospects are grim is too self-indulgent. It is true that bad news is sometimes exaggerated to frighten and then gain attention, or sales. But we need to distinguish between fear for the sake of titillation and a deepening despair that saps our power to take appropriate action.

There's a danger for average citizens to feel they've been duped too often with false alarms. I hear comments regularly: "The oil crisis in the 1970s was over much sooner than many predicted. The economy, with the help of a few minor tune-ups, has chugged along nicely ever since, thank you. We survived the cold war, and the predicted nuclear winter of the 1980s was avoided."

To be fair, it's difficult to see straight and think clearly when we're in the middle of a crisis. We tend to leave that to academics, experts, and pundits. We'd be wiser to learn from Indigenous traditions. When making long-term decisions, they peered seven generations into the past (via oral tradition) and seven generations into the future (via prayer and envisioning) to determine the decisions' likely impact.

Almost four decades ago as I scraped the pen of my alpha boar, Denzil, my old friend Lenny leaned on the steel bar (at the clean end of the pen, I noticed), and put a few thoughts out there for me to think about. "We worked harder and walked further in the 1930s than the young fellers I see today," he stated simply; and then, sensing some emphasis was warranted, he added, "Yes sirree!" and I could tell he was catching some wind for a fine tale. "We'd do chores before breakfast at seven, stook all day, and chore again before supper. I'd say we ate well, but of course that depends on whether or not you liked potatoes. To go to a party was usually a four-mile walk and then we had to get home again too, before it got too late."

"It must have been tough," I ventured.

His reply was quick. "It wasn't so bad, you know. We were all in the same boat."

"Yeah, but it was tough for all of you, wasn't it?"

"Those were the best days of my life," Lenny assured me. "We had very little, but we pulled together and had lots of fun at our parties. About all we had for music was our voices and a harmonica and I tell you, we were the best of dancers."

I thought about Lenny a few years ago when I talked to the Rotary Club in Truro, Nova Scotia, about climate change. A questioner (thank goodness for questioners) wanted to know why we should take economic risks to deal with climate change when lots of other people and other countries weren't doing the same. I suggested that we were all in the same boat, that is, Spaceship Earth. This is our living ship, named Gaia by James

Lovelock. It's up to us to live in a way to retain the regenerative capacities of Gaia. If that means reducing our GHG emissions, we should listen up. My questioner was not convinced. I realized later that the difference between Lenny and my questioner was that Lenny knew he was in the same boat with everyone else. Today we have a different impression.

It's tempting to wait until others do their share of caring for Gaia. However, we're running out of time. George Monbiot in his book *Heat* tells us we have to reduce global GHG emissions by 90 percent by 2030. Even that may be too little, too late, but it's far more than our current Canadian or global targets and certainly more than our current actions. Since 2012, Canada has been above seven hundred megatonnes CO_2 equivalent every year (Environment and Climate Change Canada, 2018). Some say we probably should emit less, but it's not fair that we do it unless everyone else does, too. Hmmm. So how long should we wait? Do we all carry on with business as usual until everyone agrees to do the right thing? Is it ethical to dodge responsibility for collective survival because others dodge?

The poorer countries on our Spaceship Earth argue that most GHG emissions benefitted the wealthier nations in the past and they, the poorer countries, have a right to catch up, even if that means burning more coal and other fossil fuels in the upcoming decades. Somehow this legitimate call for social justice must be answered. Perhaps wealthy nations have fuelled their dash to the top with GHG emissions, and to engage developing countries in the effort to rise above our global fossil-fuel addiction, Canada and other developed countries may have to reduce even more than we might otherwise calculate. Rockström et al. (2017) suggest practical ways to make it happen.

Decisions will soon change about flying, driving with cars that use excess fuel per kilometre, driving when not necessary, and adding rooms to already large houses. Today we still act as though plentiful fuel and a stable climate are our guaranteed birthright. The advent of wonky weather will eventually change how we act. However, the sooner we negotiate with each other and act as individuals, and collectively wean ourselves from fossil fuels, reduce GHG emissions, and prepare for wonky weather, the better will be our chances of living fulfilling lives into the future. Not only is today's population, whether black or white, poor or wealthy, man or woman, in the same boat, but our children, grandchildren, and all future generations of people and all living beings are in this boat. It's worth some discomfort, today, to save Spaceship Earth.

I've often wondered why there is so much resistance to walking with a lighter footprint. Why do my statements about no longer flying elicit comments such as "You're cutting off your nose to spite your face" or "Don't be unrealistic"? I can understand such volleys as "You must not value your time" or "There's no substitute for a face-to-face meeting." However, by deciding not to fly and then not flying and not spending research money for others to fly, I've noticed people imagining and implementing new ways to conduct business. There are ways to improve conference call audio quality and to link regional centres in national video conference web-links. I've also noticed how much work I can accomplish on a train or bus, without interruptions, and in the end, I often get more work done in a period before, during, and after a trip than when I drove to an airport, waited to clear security, struggled to work in narrow seats, wasted time collecting baggage at the other end, and then travelled to a city centre.

❖

Perhaps the "don't ask, don't tell" policy when we shop for cheap food or eat in restaurants and then enjoy our abundant and tasty food has its own sacred social status. While it might be considered unusual to ask about how an animal we are about to dine on was raised and slaughtered, this information and thus some relationship to the meal I ingest is crucial to how I want my life energy to be sustained. I respect the Indigenous tradition of thanking an animal for its life and life-sustaining contribution to its human predator before it is killed and carved. Authentic civility is acting with grace, when given real knowledge.

Farmers' markets are about conversations and relationships. There's nothing quite like fresh food from a vendor who can tell the story associated with it. In fact, research indicates there are far more neighbourly chats at farmers' markets, with people you choose to meet, than at supermarkets, where you might be stuck in a long line with other stranded shoppers, while waiting to go through the checkout.

Every community has special exemplars who lead in their own unique way. The Truro Farmers' Market was characterized for years by the three matriarchal mavens of the market: Greta Mathewson, Helen Bishop, and Bela Casson.

Greta sold jams, jellies, and wool products. Her comforters and mattress covers helped numerous people in the region to sleep better, and in warmth, with the thermostat turned way down. The great thing about Greta was that she loved to talk about how she and her daughter, Ruth, managed their sheep.

She could tell you about the legacy of her late husband, Bill, who built the flock and farm with Greta.

The comforters weren't just made from inert material. They were lovingly crafted from the wool of sheep well known on the farm, those animals introduced to the world by Greta, as they were born.

Greta would provide as much background as you wanted and then, with a smile, suggest you take time to think about it, or look at something slightly differently. I'm not quite sure what subliminal message she sent to me, but I never had a complete market experience without at least one jar of her jam or a package of the cards she said were "just for ewe." There was always an offer to visit their farm, a charming setting in anyone's estimation.

Helen Bishop and her husband, David, had some of the greatest chows, pickles, and relishes that a man could want. When I added a dab of Mrs. B's products to a meal, even I got compliments for my bland cooking. They bought most of their raw vegetables and fruits from other vendors at the market to keep it all local.

My daughter would laugh and remind me that Mrs. B would never accept my asking to buy just the one jar I thought I needed. More than once, I walked away lugging a small box of various jars after hearing, "You really should try these." Her smile of confidence, formed after feedback from hundreds of happy customers, convinced.

Bela Casson was a small woman, but I learned not to be fooled into thinking her size would limit her impact. She provided excellent organic vegetables to customers for years, in partnership with her husband, George, and her son, Marcus, the background-grower in their enterprise. Sadly, she passed away some time ago.

Bela could engage me in the finer points about a recent classical music concert or let me know how to contribute to a community fundraising event. This happened without a hitch as my vegetables were weighed and I was sent on my way with a smile. She was a vital member and connector in our community.

I could write about many vendors at farmers' markets. I was blessed with their perseverance and dedication to providing excellent quality at reasonable prices.

The three matriarchal mavens of the market captured my imagination. As a customer, my day, indeed my week, was improved by being the beneficiary of their knowledge and joy in providing good food and other local products. If I bought a bit too much for our household, the colourful jars circulated in the community as gifts. Each one of them could tell stories within the best tradition of Maritime lore.

These tough and gentle women earned my respect. Interestingly, even though I was a customer, I've been scolded (mildly of course) on occasion, by each of them. They knew I was hooked on their goods and would be back. They also knew me well enough to prod me to reach for higher potential, even if in simple matters. After all, it's the simple actions of our lives that add up to meaningful living and quintessence. The three mavens set examples, and if we choose to notice and follow such quiet leaders, our individual lives and communities can be richer.

Farmers' markets, community-supported agriculture, roadside stands, and similar pathways to good food help both consumers and producers to appreciate each other. To those city folks who imagine buying a small farm in case everything goes sideways, I suggest that you put effort into finding your farmer. If you choose well, and nourish the relationship, your family farmer will provide excellent value now, and in the future.

For some, God is a Stern Father and for others a Loving Mother. I've also heard reference to an Old, Aching God and, surprisingly, to a Young, Growing God. When contemplating the demise of our Earth, we can imagine the Old, Aching God of despair, who incites us to grieve. Further contemplation may also lead us to images of the Young, Growing God of hope, who delights us with possibilities. There is a temptation to resolve our uncertainty about the future by deciding to focus on either one or the other. The courageous course may be to see both the Old, Aching God and the Young, Growing God. Both, and all images of God, represent truths about ourselves, our history, and our future.

In the framework of Thomas Berry (1990), we might yet, as a species, choose to walk lightly on the path of the Ecozoic. To date, we are efficiently and somewhat blindly marching on the path of the Technozoic as if our geological impact in such a short time is negligible, in light of our accomplishments. The Old, Aching God pleads for our awareness and reorientation. The pain of past reckless deeds will always haunt, but not necessarily cripple. The Young, Growing God invites us to shift paths as she offers the Ecozoic.

As we hurtle in our compulsion to grow toward the crash at the end of our apparent r-strategy trajectory (chapter 3) of raiding, we are, arguably, realizing our fear of death. Male dominance, male violence, and authoritarianism have shaped our patterns of acquiring, warring, and exploiting (Eisler, 1987). The technologies of destruction and domination, developed under the dominator model of the hunter-warrior, are leading us to danger with predominant images of death.

Eisler's (1987) research shows that under Goddess-based religions, people lived fully enough to overcome their fear of death. In fact, in the art of these partnership periods, death was not nearly as pronounced as were symbols of supporting and enhancing life. Arguably, we have a human collective memory of celebrating life while respecting and being in balance with available resources. The apparent inevitability of an r-strategy, with economic growth as the rallying cry, can be made to yield to our faintly imprinted memories and ancient experiences of living within our means and in the joy of a k-strategy ("keepers," in chapter 3). Respecting the carrying capacity of our resource use evokes less reason for competition, hierarchical control, and wars.

Sometimes scientists, when interviewed, will be asked about the prospects for overcoming the ecological and climatic threats to our current human lifestyles. Bold interviewers will even ask about our prospects of surviving as a species. Frequently, the answer involves an assertion of optimism, with a corollary that the alternative is too awful to contemplate.

Individuals and society will be better served if we do pause to contemplate possibilities of collapse, in all their horror. Joanna Macy offers tools for us to do this in such a way that we can face despair as a genuine emotion, know it for what it is, then breathe deeply and carry on. We don't know the outcome of the human project on Planet Earth. It might fail. That acknowledgement can be grounding and empowering, leading us to a more realistic and humble assessment of how we want to redesign our relationships with each other and the living world around us.

When I was a twelve-year-old farm boy I was able to guide terrified horses from an ice-edged river in February, by holding my open palms under their chins (Martin, 2016). They responded as if being lifted by a puppet-master in the sky.

What is the nugget of spiritual insight retained by an agricultural professor who danced with horses as a boy, about five decades ago? The runaway horses experienced fear and a betrayal of trust when the traces broke, whether by poor design, neglect, or direct action. Arguably, domesticated horses, like nature, have a social-environmental contract with us, to work together in good faith, within our episodic existence, for mutual sustenance.

Our relationship to harnessed nature, within the constraints of traces to advance the human agenda, becomes strained when too much is withdrawn, or the mechanisms are poorly maintained. Wildness may erupt. The unpredictability and risk to our investment frightens us. Nature, even its domesticated species, upon escaping to wildness, elicits in us a temptation to consolidate control. The urge to clutch and pull dangling reigns breaks trust and causes resistance, whereas extended open palms of support restore relationships.

Do scientists and writers have an obligation to be reasonable, i.e., to assert only within the range of what people can accept, at the time of assertion? After all, we may turn readers off with statements deemed too difficult to consider, let alone act upon, lest current comforts and patterns be unnecessarily disrupted. In such a case, no actions will be taken, and the writer will be advised to moderate their recommendations to improve the probability of uptake. However, if we are too reasonable, readers may not understand and then not act on the crucial options that might lead us all through the darkness, when a crisis becomes more obvious.

When science leaves us at the doorstep of despair, we have so much to gain with emotional maturity, relational deepening, spiritual contemplation, and exploring ourselves through the arts. All of these can be adopted with very minimal GHG emissions. The old rock song "I can't get no satisfaction" may become "I wanna get some satisfaction." Whether Earth can retain us as a species or not, I expect it will be more satisfying to live our lives in relational, spiritual, and artistic awareness than to sink into cynicism. If our alignment with Earth is to succeed, it will be quintessential living that gets us there.

CONCLUSION

RESPECT AND GRATITUDE
FOR ENOUGH FOOD

The pursuit of ongoing growth has severe negative repercussions, and the damage affects poor people disproportionately, while the benefits accrue to wealthy people. This has resulted in increasing inequality. Oxfam (2015) reported that the poorest half of the global population, 3.5 billion-plus people, are responsible for only 10 percent of total global GHG emissions attributed to individual consumption, yet they live overwhelmingly in the countries most vulnerable to climate change.

The mantra of "feeding the world" is usually contextualized within a model of producing more and more to provide more and more. The rationale of this mantra is rooted in the Western belief in "progress," which is linked to science and reason, and is used to justify the extraction from nature of more and more materials to satisfy human needs and wants. We still tend to act as overlords of nature, to believe that we have a right to raid nature, rather than recognize our place as creatures within nature, on an Earth of interdependencies.

How then should we proceed? In previous chapters, I've noted there is mounting evidence that humanity should pull back from (1) spilling excess nitrogen and phosphorus into our biosphere, (2) displacing other species integral to ecosystem function, (3) emitting so much GHG in burning fossil fuels, (4) wasting food, (5) eating too much food and, (6) eating food that sickens us. Mayer Hillman argues it cannot be done without a collapse of civilization. He asks, "Can you see everyone in a democracy volunteering to give up flying? Can you see the majority of the population becoming vegan? Can you see the majority agreeing to restrict the size of their families?" (Barkham, 2018).

I don't know the answers to Hillman's questions. I do know that new government policies are urgently needed to ensure that we, as a society, respond quickly and in an appropriate manner to the urgent situation. Is this possible? My friend and colleague Rod MacRae of York University keeps reminding me how effectively the Canadian government responded with a food policy during the Second World War. Supply was coordinated with consumption to maintain health among Canadians. There was a collective recognition that we had a problem to address. So, it is possible to muster effective policies to deal with a crisis: we just need to agree on the challenge.

There is a temptation to believe that we can solve the problem of hunger, that we can feed the world, since humans have the technical know-how to ramp up food production. Just because we can produce more, however, it does not follow that we should. The excess food grown in the West seldom reaches those who cannot pay for it. Earth Systems have their own evolved and balanced networks of supporting life. We humans, creatures of Earth, must live within our inherited possibilities. To excessively advance our own agenda at the expense of the Earth agenda is to harm ourselves. This harm, and it will take place, may occur in millennia, or in centuries; but at this point it seems likely that it will take place in only decades.

Current corporate bosses have an inordinate focus on quarterly profits, partly because their shareholders expect high returns and partly because there are so many opportunities for them to accumulate cash and stock options in their personal accounts. Not only does the existing system reward corporate bosses for pursuing short-term gains, it generates excess money from the destructive extraction of natural resources. It makes no sense that those individuals should "earn" one hundred to three hundred times more than an average worker in annual salaries and benefits. There is a case to be made for lessening the pay of corporate bosses by an order of magnitude, making it ten to thirty times the average worker's pay at most. I'm anticipating a news story about executives who cap their salaries at thirty times the average wage and put any additional remuneration offered into an environmental contingency fund. That is twenty-first century leadership waiting to happen.

We might accept that the corporate agenda is not so much a sinister plot as it is a *modus operandi* that evolved as selected decision-makers, in boardrooms, crafted and polished systems that worked. Given the urgent state of things, the present response of Earth and the expected response of Earth to the plundering of it, and the fact that there will be more and more harm to humans, we can surmise that current corporate craftsmanship will just keep on working, until it doesn't.

The wealth created by businesses and industry has contributed significantly to human well-being. However, as noted, that wealth has been created at great environmental cost and the wealth created has not been shared equitably. A great deal of work needs to be done to achieve social justice and proper respect for the environment. The promise of wealth, the goods and services, the employment and pension plans offered by corporations are seductive. A powerful fantasy has been created and it is now believed to be true by most; we assume we now understand reality. Corporations and their accoutrements are only a human construct, however. That we accept raiding of Earth to the extent we have, indicates we have allowed this human construct to capture and subdue our imaginations. Tragically, this is occurring just when we need as much holistic imagination as possible. Now is the time for as many people as possible to show up with emotional, spiritual, intellectual, and relational maturity. Too much deference to a corporate rationale is to diminish ourselves and our chances for meeting Anthropocene challenges.

With greater fiscal prudence, we would be able to sustain dynamic stability. Can we imagine a restored economic system that allows new technologies to emerge and thrive, that conserves energy and generates it, with much less impact than fossil-fuel burning? This same system could be guided by policies to strategically phase out polluting technology. This system of dynamic stability would not be predicated on growth, but on the production of goods and services of benefit to people, Earth, and future generations. The focus would be to drop what is not of benefit and to profitably pick up what is of benefit.

Wendell Berry (2000) reflected on the lessons he learned by being observant on his home farm.

> I see the life of this place [the home farm] is always emerging beyond expectation or prediction or typicality, that is unique, given to the world minute by minute, only once, never to be repeated. And then is when I see that this life is a miracle, absolutely worth having, absolutely worth saving.

Berry has a relationship with his farm, as most farm people do, especially if their families have been on the same land over generations. In every class, I ask my students which generation they represent on their home farm. There are many who are third- and fourth-generation farmers, a few Maritime students are the eighth generation, and one Ontario student was the ninth generation. In an exceptional situation, a student from Europe was at least the sixteenth generation on his farm and he didn't know if he still wanted to farm. Imagine the conversations between generations fifteen and sixteen. I know a sixth-generation farmer who is keenly aware that his ancestors are buried on the farm, and I'm wondering if that is their not-so-subtle reminder that the land is to be sustained for agriculture. The family observations, sacrifices, joys, stories, and visceral connection to a home farm are to be treasured.

When I attend farm meetings, and gaze at the capacity and knowledge in the room, I wonder how many of today's farmers have ancestors who escaped to North America from the clearances in Scotland, from the potato famine in Ireland, from the persecution of Mennonites in Europe, Russia, and Ukraine, from the horrors of the First World War and the Second World War, and from other global oppression. If our ancestors could talk to us as aggies about how we have become vulnerable to excess debt, and to the influence of just a few corporations in agriculture, what would they advise? Surely not to become more vulnerable. Who mostly benefits from the myth that farmers should grow more and more? In the meantime, we are eating ourselves sick and wasting food as if it is too cheap and too plentiful.

It is the logic of growth that has brought us to where we are — mere tweaking of that system will only dig us in deeper. It is now time to transcend growth and to organize ourselves to appreciate who we are, in the first quarter of the twenty-first century. We need Earth Systems to function. We are not components of economic systems but rather creatures evolved from stardust, with ancestors who understood their place in the cosmos and Earth. Our children and descendants are counting on us to recognize who we are, and who we are not, at this pivotal point. We are no longer ignorant about our impact on Earth and on fellow creatures — we know what we do. The luxury of being too busy, too preoccupied, too paralyzed, too comfortable, or too confused about how to address our impact are now unaffordable extravagances.

Joanna Macy would probably exhort me to be more gracious in my previous statement. When I was in her workshop, in 2006, at the Tatamagouche Centre in Nova Scotia, she helped us perceive how the disconnects of modern life can result in a descent into despair. I learned that while grieving for the current conditions on Earth is appropriate, it is important to see that, having grieved, there is an opportunity to do what needs doing to correct the damage, regardless how small the act.

> The viciousness and brutality that have always been with us are so obvious now, and although terrifying, they're right up front for all to see. Their currency is fear — fear that distorts and deadens the mind. And now it's clear: love must, and can, triumph over fear. If we're not up for love yet — and a lot of the time I feel I'm not — we can lean into trust. That's something I can do. I can learn to trust, and I'm doing that. (Macy, 2018)

Many Indigenous Peoples retain knowledge of an Earth-based spirituality and the settlers who have lost ancestral appreciation to recover this may be able to recover it from them. Their emphasis is not about a hierarchy of God over man over nature, as I was taught in my undergrad philosophy classes, but is more about how humans are creatures, within and part of Creation. The option to be grateful, with such spiritual, emotional, and intellectual awareness, is compelling.

Indigenous Peoples have survived so much devastation to their civilizations, communities, and individuals. They have lessons to teach all of us about what is most important and crucial for survival.

I'll never forget the day Albert Marshall, a Mi'kmaq elder, accepted my invitation to talk to faculty and students at our agricultural campus in Truro, Nova Scotia. He talked about the promise of two-eyed seeing — one eye of Indigenous knowledge and one eye of scientific knowledge. Each eye contributes to how we know the world, but why keep one eye shut? And he kept talking, without notes, as he sat on the edge of a desk, long beyond the assigned time for the seminar. I was worried that audience members were being polite and wanted to leave and so, as the facilitator, I gave them the option. No one left. "Both eyes should be wide open," Albert told us, and then provided example after example, replete with wisdom embedded in stories.

Although Albert had examples, it is my young colleague Kerdo who practically helped me appreciate the potential for two-eyed seeing. In his early thirties, with traditional knowledge from his elders, and also with scientific knowledge from modern education, he is leading an initiative at the Kayanase Greenhouse in Ohsweken, Ontario, to propagate and nurture native plant species from his community. The goal is to restore the presence of some of these species, which the Indigenous Peoples value for food and medicine, in the context of biodiversity in the surrounding habitat. Kerdo asks very appropriate questions about how climate change may impact the efforts and how species populations shift over time. What implications does that have for their community of people and plants?

A more radical approach — radical, both in the sense of "proceeding from a root" and of being seen as "extreme" — was to grant a New Zealand river the same rights as humans. The worldview of the Whanganui iwi is to treat the river as a living entity, as an indivisible whole, rather than owning and managing it (Roy, 2017). If I was a betting man, I would bet that our survival as a human species will be further advanced by granting these rights to rivers, rather than to corporations, with their awe-insisting cathedrals of glass and steel.

Perhaps the grace of the twenty-first century is that even today "the world's Indigenous groups … manage 80 per cent of Earth's biodiversity, in part because their ancestral lands make up 22 per cent of the world's land surface" (Chellaney, 2019). We need their husbanding, their traditional knowledge, and their model of respect for Earth.

For years I have meditatively walked the Stations of the Cosmos spiral behind the greenhouse at the Ignatius Jesuit Centre, just outside Guelph. Based on the writings of Thomas Berry, the first station, in the centre of the spiral, represents the great flaring forth. Berry was a man who used language to help us envision the wonder of the universe story. After one walks, stopping at stations celebrating stages of the universe and of Earth, the last station positions the walker in "this present moment of grace." Indeed, we still have grace, at this stage of the long journey, and can choose to live within Earth System reality.

Spirituality provides more than an eternal life insurance policy, allowing believers to escape this world and flourish in the next. Our spirituality can be rooted in previous human understandings of our place in Creation and can be aspirational about how we may deepen our wisdom and humility as we participate in a creative process, with full understanding of who we are, and how we relate to Earth and the Cosmos.

Pierre Teilhard de Chardin is well known for saying that "We are not human beings having a spiritual experience; we are spiritual beings having a human experience." It is our great privilege to be here, now, participating in the ongoing emergence of Earth.

Our spiritual understanding and our scientific knowing can reinforce one another and our relationship to science must mature beyond our child-like curiosity about technological possibilities. Science can help us understand the value of adaptive ecosystem design over millennia and how we can participate within and not against the evolving process.

Science is about the research questions we ask and the hypotheses we choose to test. We can choose to advance inquiries about our place in the interdependent web of life and we can choose to seek answers to gaining power over Earth Systems, for now. Science is being sold short, if used only to develop more technology, especially if the technology is not used for actual human needs and within Earth System networks. Science can help us understand how Earth Systems function. We can learn how to live and sustain ourselves within resilient ecosystems.

Research in space is providing more practical options for living without waste and in a recycling economy on a space station. We can learn to apply these skills on Spaceship Earth.

Food viscerally connects us to Earth. Food production, provision, and preparation involve human awareness and agency. Our food awareness and agency were fundamental to traditional cultures, have culturally evolved among individuals and communities, could be essential components of our current education curriculums, and should not be surrendered lightly. To give up food awareness and agency or to never claim them is to be vulnerable and less conscious of who we are and how we connect to Earth. To rely too much on businesses, providing food convenience, is to risk giving up essential knowledge and skills.

Since the industrial revolution we have relied on economic growth as a rising tide to lift all boats. We may not have been expected to know then what we know now. However, now we are aware that the mantra of growth led to raiding Earth and to the profligacy of excess and waste. In this present moment of grace, we are well advised to let go of our attachment to growth and to hold out our upward-facing palms in gratitude; gratitude for the journey of the universe and of Earth to provide life in all its beauty, gratitude for all our relations, and gratitude for the food of Earth which sustains us. Excess is yesterday's notion. Being grateful for enough is the assurance of today and tomorrow.

ACKNOWLEDGEMENTS

It was from my Grampa, as we did our chores on the farm, that I fundamentally learned about respect; respect for soil, respect for plants, respect for animals, both in the barn, and those outside, who walk, crawl, fly, and swim. He didn't talk much and died when I was seven. The rest of my knowledge, mostly details about the systems of agriculture and ecology, was built on his foundational influence.

The material and ideas in this book were formed under the influence of numerous colleagues, students, farmers, authors, scientists, relatives, and friends. I haven't kept track of the details of how my understanding of food security evolved. I know that I am a student of everyone I encounter. I appreciate those who disagree with me, because they help me to deliberate and reconsider. I appreciate those who are supportive, because they encourage me when I hesitate. I appreciate those who are neutral, because they compel me to speak up.

BIBLIOGRAPHY

African Orphan Crops Consortium (AOCC). "About." 2019. africanorphancrops.org/about/.

Allen, Myles R., Opha Pauline Dube, William Solecki, Fernando Aragon-Durand, Wolfgang Cramer, Stephen Humphreys, Mikiko Kainuma, et al. "Framing and Context." In *Global Warming of 1.5°C: An IPCC Special Report on the Impacts of Global Warming of 1.5°C Above Pre-Industrial Levels and Related Global Greenhouse Gas Emission Pathways in the Context of Strengthening the Global Response to the Threat of Climate Change, Sustainable Development, and Efforts to Eradicate Poverty*, edited by V. Masson-Delmotte, P. Zhai, H. O. Pörtner, D. Roberts, J. Skea, P. R. Shukla, A. Pirani, et al., 49–91. Geneva: The Intergovernmental Panel on Climate Change (IPCC), October 8, 2018. ipcc.ch/sr15/chapter/chapter-1-pdf/.

Associated Press. "Forget Crops — Farmers in Dry California Sell Their Water."

Bak, Celine. "Why Climate Risk Disclosure Is Key to a Sustainable Economy." Media Planet insert, *National Post*, December 17, 2018. industryandbusiness.ca/insight/why-climate-risk-disclosure-is-key-to-a-sustainable-economy.

Barkham, Patrick. "'We're Doomed': Mayer Hillman on the Climate Reality No One Else Will Dare Mention." *Guardian*, April 26, 2018. theguardian.com/environment/2018/apr/26/were-doomed-mayer-hillman-on-the-climate-reality-no-one-else-will-dare-mention.

Bartels, Jos, and Isabelle van den Berg. "Fresh Fruit and Vegetables and the Added Value of Antioxidants." *British Food Journal* 113, no. 11 (2011): 1339–52. doi.org/10.1108/00070701111179979.

Beach, Heather M., Ken W. Laing, Morris Van De Walle, and Ralph C. Martin. "The Current State and Future Directions of Organic No-Till Farming with Cover Crops in Canada, with Case Study Support." *Sustainability* 10, no. 2 (January 2018): 373. doi.org/10.3390/su10020373.

Berry, Thomas. *The Dream of the Earth*. San Francisco: Sierra Club, 1990.

Berry, Wendell. *Life Is a Miracle: An Essay Against Modern Superstition*. Washington, DC: Counterpoint Press, 2000.

Best, Peter. "Poultry Performance Improves Over Past Decades." *WattAgNet*, November 24, 2011. wattagnet.com/articles/10427-poultry-performance-improves-over-past-decades.

Black, Harvey. "Black Soldier Flies as Recyclers of Waste." *Entomology Today*, May 26, 2015. entomologytoday.org/2015/05/26/black-soldier-flies-as-recyclers-of-waste-and-possible-livestock-feed/.

Borken-Kleefeld, Jens, Terje Bernsten, and Jan Fuglestvedt. "Specific Climate Impact of Passenger and Freight Transport." *Environmental Science and Technology* 44, no. 15 (July 2010): 5700–06. pubs.acs.org/doi/10.1021/es9039693.

Boseley, Sarah. "Global Cost of Obesity-Related Illness to Hit $1.2tn a Year from 2025." *Guardian*, October 10, 2017. theguardian.com/society/2017/oct/10/treating-obesity-related-illness-will-cost-12tn-a-year-from-2025-experts-warn.

Boulding, Kenneth. In United States Congress, House (1973), *Energy Reorganization Act of 1973: Hearings*, Ninety-Third Congress, First Session, on H.R. 11510.

Brown, Christine. "Soil Organic Matter in Ontario." Ontario Ministry of Agriculture, Food and Rural Affairs (OMAFRA), 2017.

Bruening, Meg, Richard MacLehose, Katie Loth, Mary Story, and Dianne Neumark-Sztainer. "Feeding a Family in a Recession: Food Insecurity Among Minnesota Parents." *American Journal of Public Health* 102, no. 3 (January 2012): 520–26. ajph.aphapublications.org/doi/10.2105/AJPH.2011.300390.

Buchanan, Mark. "The Science of Inequality." *New Statesman*, September 2, 2002. newstatesman.com/node/156183.

Buffett, Howard G., and Howard W. Buffett. "Souped-Up Yields from Stripped-Down Tools." In *Forty Chances: Finding Hope in a Hungry World*. New York: Simon & Schuster, 2013.

ChangeLab Solutions. *Breaking Down the Chain: A Guide to the Soft Drink Industry*. Oakland: ChangeLab Solutions, 2012. changelabsolutions.org/sites/default/files/ChangeLab-Beverage_Industry_Report-FINAL_201109.pdf.

Chellaney, Brahma. "Indigenous Groups Are the World's Endangered Environmental Guardians." *Globe and Mail*, January 11, 2019. theglobeandmail.com/opinion/article-indigenous-groups-are-the-worlds-endangered-environmental-guardians/.

Crews, T. E., and Mark B. Peoples. "Legume Versus Fertilizer Sources of Nitrogen: Ecological Tradeoffs and Human Needs." *Agriculture, Ecosystems & Environment* 102, no. 3 (May 2004): 279–97. doi.org/10.1016/j.agee.2003.09.018.

de Ponti, Tomek, Bert Rijk, and Martin K. van Ittersum. "The Crop Yield Gap Between Organic and Conventional Agriculture."*Agricultural Systems* 108 (April 2012): 1–9. doi.org/10.1016/j.agsy.2011.12.004.

Ding, Ting, Barbara Mullan, and Kristina Xavier. "Does Subjective Well-Being Predict Health-Enhancing Behaviour? The Example of Fruit and Vegetable Consumption." *British Food Journal* 116, no. 4 (2014): 598–610. doi.org/10.1108/BFJ-07-2012-0177.

Dostoyevsky, Fyodor. *The Brothers Karamazov*. Markham, ON: Penguin Books, 1975.

Douthwaite, Richard. *The Growth Illusion*. Tulsa, OK: Council Oak Books, 1992.

Drengson, Alan. "The Life and Work of Arne Naess: An Appreciative Overview." *The Trumpeter* 21, no. 1 (2005): 6–47.

Drinkwater, Laurie E., Peggy Wagoner, and Marianne Sarrantonio. "Legume-Based Cropping Systems Have Reduced Carbon and N Losses." *Nature* 396 (November 1998): 262–65. doi.org/10.1038/24376.

Dubé, Laurette, Paul Thomassin, Janet Beauvais, and David Sparling. "Building Convergence: Toward an Integrated

Health & AgriFood Strategy for Canada." Ottawa: Canadian Agri-food Policy Institute (CAPI), 2009. capi-icpa.ca/wp-content/uploads/2009/08/Building-Convergence-Toward-an-Integrated-Health-and-Agri-Food-Strategy-for-Canada-2009.pdf.

Dukes, Jeffrey S., Jennifer Pontius, David Orwig, Jeffrey R. Garnas, Vikki L. Rodgers, Nicholas Brazee, Barry Coke, et al. "Responses of Insect Pests, Pathogens, and Invasive Plant Species to Climate Change in the Forests of Northeastern North America: What Can We Predict?" *Canadian Journal of Forest Research* 39, no. 2 (February 2009): 231–48. doi.org/10.1139/X08-171.

Eilers, W., R. MacKay, L. Graham, and A. Lefebvre, eds. "Environmental Sustainability of Canadian Agriculture: Agri-Environmental Indicator Report Series — Report #3." Ottawa: Agriculture and Agri-Food Canada, 2010: 235.

Eisler, Riane. *The Chalice and the Blade*. New York: HarperCollins, 1987.

Elliot, Larry. "World's 26 Richest People Own as Much as Poorest 50%, Says Oxfam." *Guardian*, January 21, 2019. theguardian.com/business/2019/jan/21/world-26-richest-people-own-as-much-as-poorest-50-per-cent-oxfam-report.

Environment and Climate Change Canada. "Canadian Environmental Sustainability Indicators: Greenhouse Gas Emissions." Gatineau, QC: Environment and Climate Change Canada, 2018. canada.ca/en/environment-climate-change/services/environmental-indicators/greenhouse-gas-emissions.html.

Erisman, Jan Willem, Mark A. Sutton, James Galloway, Zbigniew Klimont, and Wilfried Winiwarter. "How a

Century of Ammonia Synthesis Changed the World." *Nature Geoscience* 1, no. 10 (2008): 636–39.

Field to Market: The Alliance for Sustainable Agriculture. "Environmental and Socioeconomic Indicators for Measuring Outcomes of On-Farm Agricultural Production in the United States: Summary Report (Version 2)." December 2012. aae.wisc.edu/aae375/sustainable_ag/ Environmental%20and%20Socioeconomic%20Indicators %20for%20MeasuringOutcomes%20of%20OnFarm%20 Ag%20Production%202012%20Field%20to%20 Market%20Report.pdf.

Florida, Richard, Charlotta Mellander, and Karen M. King. "The Global Creativity Index, 2015." Toronto: Martin Prosperity Institute, University of Toronto, Rotman School of Management, 2015. martinprosperity.org/content/ the-global-creativity-index-2015/.

Food and Agriculture Organization of the United Nations (FAO). "AGP — Food Security." 2019. fao.org/agricul- ture/crops/thematic-sitemap/theme/spi/soil-biodiversity/ effect-of-human-activity-on-biodiversity/food-security/en/.

———. "Livestock a Major Threat to Environment." Rome: Food and Agriculture Organization of the United Nations, FAO Newsroom, November 29, 2006. fao.org/newsroom/ en/news/2006/1000448/.

———. "Policy Support and Governance: Sustainable Intensification of Agriculture." n.d. fao.org/policy-support/ policy-themes/sustainable-intensification-agriculture/ en/.

Freemark, Kathryn E., and David A. Kirk. "Birds on Organic and Conventional Farms in Ontario: Partitioning Effects of Habitat and Practices on Species Composition and Abundance." *Biological Conservation* 101, no. 3 (October 2001): 337–50. doi.org/10.1016/S0006-3207(01)00079-9.

Fry, Robert C. "Measuring Feed Efficiency: Why & How on the Back of a Napkin." *Florida Ruminant Nutrition Symposia* 60 (2011): 17–19.

Gaudin, Amélie C. M., Sabrina Westra, Cora E. S. Loucks, Ken Janovicek, Ralph C. Martin, and William Deen. "Improving Resilience of Northern Field Crop Systems Using Inter-Seeded Red Clover: A Review." *Agronomy* 3, no. 1 (February 2013): 148–180. doi.org/10.3390/agronomy3010148.

Gaudin, Amélie C. M., Tor N. Tolhurst, Alan P. Ker, Ken Janovicek, Cristina Tortora, Ralph C. Martin, and William Deen. "Increasing Crop Diversity Mitigates Weather Variations and Improves Yield Stability." *PLOS ONE* 10, no. 2 (February 2015). doi.org/10.1371/journal.pone.0113261.

Girard, Judith, Pierre Mineau, and Lenore Fahrig. "Higher Nestling Food Biomass in Organic than Conventional Soybean Fields in Eastern Ontario, Canada." *Agriculture, Ecosystems & Environment* 189 (May 2014): 199–205. doi.org/10.1016/j.agee.2014.03.033.

Gooch, Martin, and Abdel Felfel. "'$27 Billion' Revisited: The Cost of Canada's Annual Food Waste." Edited by Caroline Glasbey. Oakville, ON: Value Chain Management International Inc, 2014. vcm-international.com/wp-content/uploads/2014/12/Food-Waste-in-Canada-27-Billion-Revisited-Dec-10-2014.pdf.

Gooch, Martin, Delia Bucknell, Dan Laplain, Benjamin Dent, Peter Whitehead, and Abdel Felfel. "The Avoidable

Crisis of Food Waste." Edited by Caroline Glasbey. Oakville, ON: Value Chain Management International and Second Harvest, 2019. secondharvest.ca/research/the-avoidable-crisis-of-food-waste/.

Gornall, Jemma, Richard Betts, Eleanor Burke, Robin Clark, Joanne Camp, Kate Willett, and Andrew Wiltshire. "Implications of Climate Change for Agricultural Productivity in the Early Twenty-First Century." *Philosophic Transactions of the Royal Society B Biological Sciences* 365, no. 1554 (2010): 2973–89.

Graves, Margaret E., and Ralph C. Martin. "Grassland Management to Minimize the Environmental Impact of Dairy Farming." In *Achieving Sustainable Production of Milk Volume 2: Safety, Quality and Sustainability*, edited by Nico van Belzen. Cambridge, UK: Burleigh Dodds Science Publishing, 2017.

Grooten, Monique, and Rosamunde Almond, eds. "Living Planet Report— 2018: Aiming Higher." Gland, Switzerland: World Wildlife Foundation, 2018. wwf.panda.org/knowledge_hub/all_publications/living_planet_report_2018/

Group, Edward. "Soft Drinks: America's Other Drinking Problem." Global Healing Centre, March 17, 2016. globalhealingcenter.com/natural-health/soft-drinks-americas-other-drinking-problem/.

Hamzelou, Jessica. "Overeating Now Bigger Global Problem than Lack of Food." *New Scientist*, December 13, 2012. newscientist.com/article/dn23004-overeating-now-bigger-global-problem-than-lack-of-food/.

Harari, Yuval Noah. *21 Lessons for the 21st Century*. London: Jonathan Cape, 2018.

Hawken, Paul. *Blessed Unrest.* New York: Viking Press, 2007.

Heart and Stroke Foundation of Canada. "The Kids Are Not Alright: How the Food and Beverage Industry Is Marketing Our Children and Youth to Death: 2017 Report on the Health of Canadians." February 1, 2017. heartandstroke. ca/-/media/pdf-files/canada/2017-heart-month/heartand-stroke-reportonhealth2017.ashx?la=en&hash=1D-4354193C46A235D2A657230FE2EB29DC6F34C8.

Herbert, Georgia, Laurie Butler, Orla Kennedy, and Alexandra Lobb. "Young UK Adults and the 5 A DAY Campaign: Perceived Benefits and Barriers of Eating More Fruits and Vegetables." *International Journal of Consumer Studies* 34, no. 6 (November 2010): 657–64. doi. org/10.1111/j.1470-6431.2010.00872.x.

Hesse, Hermann Karl. *Siddhartha: A New Translation.* Boston: Shambala Press, 2000.

Hirel, Bertrand, Jacques Le Gouis, Bertrand Ney, and André Gallais. "The Challenge of Improving Nitrogen Use Efficiency in Crop Plants: Towards a More Central Role for Genetic Variability and Quantitative Genetics Within Integrated Approaches." *Journal of Experimental Botany* 58, no. 9 (July 2007): 2369–87. doi.org/10.1093/jxb/erm097.

Hirschfeld, Sarah E. "Characterizing Plant Communities on Canadian Permaculture Farms." Master's thesis. Guelph: University of Guelph, 2017.

Hoegh-Guldberg, Ove, Daniela Jacob, Michael Taylor, Marco Bindi, Sally Brown, Ines Camilloni, Arona Diedhiou, et al. "Impacts of 1.5°C Global Warming on Natural and Human Systems." In *Global Warming of 1.5°C: An IPCC*

Special Report on the Impacts of Global Warming of 1.5°C Above Pre-Industrial Levels and Related Global Greenhouse Gas Emission Pathways in the Context of Strengthening the Global Response to the Threat of Climate Change, Sustainable Development, and Efforts to Eradicate Poverty, edited by V. Masson-Delmotte, P. Zhai, H. O. Pörtner, D. Roberts, J. Skea, P.R. Shukla, A. Pirani, et al., 175–311. Geneva: The Intergovernmental Panel on Climate Change (IPCC), October 9, 2018. ipcc.ch/site/assets/uploads/sites/2/2019/02/SR15_Chapter3_Low_Res.pdf.

Homer-Dixon, Thomas. *The Upside of Down*. Toronto: Vintage Canada, 2007.

Igbozurike, Matthias U. "Ecological Balance in Tropical Agriculture." *Geographical Review* 61, no. 4 (October 1971): 519–29.

Insurance Bureau of Canada (IBC). "2018 Facts of the Property and Casualty Insurance Industry in Canada." Toronto: Insurance Bureau of Canada (IBC), 2018. assets.ibc.ca/Documents/Facts%20Book/Facts_Book/2018/IBC-Fact-Book-2018.pdf.

Kimmerer, Robin Wall. *Braiding Sweetgrass*. Minneapolis: Milkweed Editions, 2013.

Kirkpatrick, Sharon I., and Valerie Tarasuk. "Food Insecurity Is Associated with Nutrient Inadequacies Among Canadian Adults and Adolescents." *Journal of Nutrition* 138, no. 3 (April 2008): 604–12.

Kummu, M., H. de Moel, M. Porkka, S. Siebert, O. Varis, and P. J. Ward. "Lost Food, Wasted Resources: Global Food Supply Chain Losses and Their Impacts on Freshwater, Cropland, and Fertiliser Use." *Science of the Total Environment* 438 (November 2012): 477–89. doi.org/10.1016/j.scitotenv.2012.08.092.

Kuntsler, James Howard. *The Long Emergency*. New York: Grove Press, 2006.

Lampkin, Nicolas. *Organic Farming*. Ipswich, UK: Organic Farming Press, 1990.

Laraia, Barbara A. "Food Insecurity and Chronic Disease." *Advances in Nutrition* 4, no. 2 (March 2013): 203–12. doi. org/10.3945/an.112.003277.

Li, Yinpeng, Wei Ye, Meng Wang, and Xiaodong Yan. "Climate Change and Drought: A Risk Assessment of Crop-Yield Impacts." *Climate Research* 39, no. 1 (May 2009): 31–46.

Lightburn, Kyra K., Ralph C. Martin, and Nigel E. Raine. "The Effects of Grassland Management on Wild Bees in Rotationally Grazed Pastures in Southern Ontario." Poster presented at the Entomological Society of Canada and America Joint Annual Meeting, Vancouver, BC, November 11–14, 2018.

Lister, Bradford C., and Andres Garcia. "Climate-Driven Declines in Arthropod Abundance Restructure a Rainforest Food Web." *Proceedings of the National Academy Sciences of the United States of America* (*PNAS*) 115, no. 44 (October 2018). doi.org/10.1073/pnas.1722477115.

Lutz, Wolfgang, Bill Butz, Samir K. C., Warren Sanderson, and Sergei Scherbov. "9 Billion or 11 Billion? The Research Behind New Population Projections." *Nexus: The Research Blog of IIASA* (blog). International Institute for Applied Systems Analysis, September 23, 2014. blog.iiasa. ac.at/2014/09/23/9-billion-or-11-billion-the-research-be-hind-new-population-projections/.

Lynch, Derek H., Roderick John MacRae, and Ralph C. Martin. "The Carbon and Global Warming Potential Impacts of

Organic Farming: Does It Have a Significant Role in an Energy Constrained World?" *Sustainability* 3, no. 2 (January 2011): 322–62. doi.org/10.3390/su3020322.

Lynch, Derek H., Jennifer Sumner, and Ralph C. Martin. "Framing the Social, Ecological and Economic Goods and Services Derived from Organic Agriculture in the Canadian Context." In *Organic Farming, Prototype for Sustainable Agriculture*, edited by Stéphane Bellon and Servane Penvern, 347–65. New York: Springer Science+Business Media Dordrecht, 2014. doi.org/10.1007/978-94-007-7927-3_19.

Macy, Joanna. *Letter from Joanna, May 2018*. May 24, 2018. workthatreconnects.org/letter-from-joanna-may-2018/.

Main, M., Mark Juhasz, and Ralph C. Martin. Review of "Sustainability Indicators of Dairying in Ontario." Agriculture and Agri-Food Canada, March, 2012: 50.

Martin, Ralph C. "The Application of Deep Ecology in Cuba." *The Trumpeter* 16, no. 1 (2000): 1–7. trumpeter.athabascau.ca/index.php/trumpet/article/view/148/177.

Martin, Ralph C. "Horses in the River." *Rhubarb* 38 (Winter 2016): 14–15.

Martin, Ralph C., Thor J. Arnason, John D. H. Lambert, Pierre Isabelle, Harvey D. Voldeng, and Donald L. Smith. "Reduction of European Corn Borer (Lepidoptera: Pyralidae) Damage by Intercropping Corn with Soybean." *Journal of Economic Entomology* 82, no. 5 (October 1989): 1455–59. doi.org/10.1093/jee/82.5.1455.

Martin, Ralph C., Tess Astatkie, and Julia M. Cooper. "The Effect of Soybean Variety on Corn Soybean Intercrop Biomass and Protein Yields." *Canadian Journal of Plant Science* 78, no. 2 (1998): 289–94. doi.org/10.4141/P97-030.

Martin, Ralph C., Harvey D. Voldeng, and Donald L. Smith. "Intercropping Corn and Soybean for Silage in a Cool Temperature Region: Yield, Protein and Economic Benefits." *Field Crops Research* 23, no. 3–4 (June 1990): 295–310.

———. "Nitrogen Transfer from Nodulating Soybean to Maize or to Nonnodulating Soybean in Intercrops: The 15N Dilution Method." *Plant and Soil* 132, no. 1 (April 1991): 53–63. doi.org/10.1007/BF00011012.

Mathews, Justin. "The Fact Sheet: Prepare to Be Amazed by Canada's Agricultural Industry." *TalentEgg*, February 16, 2015. talentegg.ca/incubator/2015/02/16/fact-sheet-canadas-agriculture-industry/.

Melville, Herman. *Moby Dick*. Hungary: Konemann, 1995.

Milman, Oliver, and Stuart Leavenworth. "China's Plan to Cut Meat Consumption by 50% Cheered by Climate Campaigners." *Guardian*, June 20, 2016. theguardian.com/world/2016/jun/20/chinas-meat-consumption-climate-change.

Monbiot, George. *Heat: How We Can Stop the Planet Burning*. Toronto: Doubleday Canada, 2006.

———. "In this Age of Diamond Saucepans, Only a Recession Makes Sense." *Guardian*, October 8, 2007.

———. "Materialism: A System that Eats Us From the Inside Out." *Guardian Weekly*, December 9, 2013. theguardian.com/commentisfree/2013/dec/09/materialism-system-eats-us-from-inside-out.

———. "Rich Can't Blame the Poor for the P-Word." *Guardian Weekly*, February 8, 2008.

———. "We Should Welcome a Recession." *Guardian Weekly*, October 12, 2007.

Moyer, Jeff. *Organic No-Till Farming*. Austin: Acres USA, 2011.

Muggah, Robert. "Tackling Global Problems? Look to Cities, Not Countries." *Globe and Mail*, June 17, 2017. theglobeandmail.com/opinion/tackling-global-problems-look-to-cities-not-countries/article35330858/.

Muller, Adrian, Christian Schader, Nadia El-Hage Scialabba, Judith Brüggemann, Anne Isensee, Karl-Heinz Erb, Pete Smith, et al. "Strategies for Feeding the World More Sustainably with Organic Agriculture." *Nature Communications* 8 (November 2017): 1290. doi.org/10.1038/s41467-017-01410-w.

National Cancer Institute. "Acrylamide and Cancer Risk." *National Cancer Institute*, December 5, 2017. cancer.gov/about-cancer/causes-prevention/risk/diet/acrylamide-fact-sheet.

Neate, Rupert. "World's Richest 500 See Their Wealth Increase by $1tn This Year." *Guardian*, December 27, 2017. theguardian.com/inequality/2017/dec/27/worlds-richest-500-see-increased-their-wealth-by-1tn-this-year.

Nickerson, Mike. *Life, Money and Illusion: Living on Earth as if We Want to Stay*. Lanark, ON: Seven Generations Publishing, 2006.

Nielsen, Robert L. "Historical Corn Grain Yields for the U.S." West Lafayette, IN: Agronomy Department, Purdue University, 2017. agry.purdue.edu/ext/corn/news/timeless/YieldTrends.html.

Niviana, Aka, and Kathy Jetnil-Kijiner. Poem quoted in "A Cost Only Art Can Measure" by Bill McKibben. *Sojourners* 47, no. 10 (November 2018): 23.

Novacek, Michael J. "Engaging the Public on Biodiversity Issues." *Proceedings of the National Academy Sciences of the United States of America* (*PNAS*), 105 (August 2008): 11562–78. doi.org/10.1073/pnas.0802599105.

———. "It Happened to Him. It's Happening to You." *Washington Post*, January 13, 2008. washingtonpost.com/wp-dyn/content/article/2008/01/11/AR2008011101994.html?noredirect=on.

Ogilvie, Cameron Mark, William Deen, and Ralph C. Martin. "Service Crop Management to Maximize Crop Water Supply and Improve Agroecosystem Resilience: A Review." *Journal of Soil Water Conservation* 74:389–404. doi:10.2489/jswc.74.4.389

Ontario Ministry of Agriculture, Food and Rural Affairs (OMAFRA). "New Horizons: Ontario's Agricultural Soil Health and Conservation Strategy." 2018. omafra.gov.on.ca/english/landuse/soil-strategy.htm.

Ontario Ministry of Agriculture, Food and Rural Affairs (OMAFRA). "Regulatory Requirements for On-Farm Anaerobic Digestion Facilities under Ontario Regulation 267/03." 2016. omafra.gov.on.ca/english/engineer/facts/nm_ad.htm.

Oxfam. "Extreme Carbon Inequality." Oxfam Media Briefing, December 2, 2015.

Parizeau, Kate, Mike Von Massow, and Ralph C. Martin. "Household-Level Dynamics of Food Waste Production and Related Beliefs, Attitudes, and Behaviours in Guelph, Ontario." *Waste Management* 35 (January 2015): 207–17. doi.org/10.1016/j.wasman.2014.09.019.

Pilger, Gerald. "Farm Debt Ratio in Canada Could Create an Agricultural 'Bust.'" *Country Guide*, November 26, 2014. country-guide.ca/guide-business/farm-debt-ratio-in-canada-could-create-an-agricultural-bust-scenario.

Pilkington, Ed. "Trump Administration's Opposition to Breastfeeding Resolution Sparks Outrage." *Guardian*, July 8, 2018. theguardian.com/us-news/2018/jul/08/trump-administration-opposes-breastfeeding-resolution-report?utm_source=esp&utm_medium=Email&utm_campaign=GU+Today+main+NEW+H+categories&utm_term=280531&subid=21198872&CMP=EMCNEWEML6619I2.

Pimentel, D., J. Allen, A. Beers, L. Guinand, R. Linder, P. McLaughlin, B. Meer, et al. "World Agriculture and Soil Erosion." *BioScience* 37, no. 4 (April 1987): 277–83. doi.org/10.2307/1310591.

Pollan, Michael. *In Defense of Food: An Eater's Manifesto*. New York: Penguin, 2008.

Pope Francis. "*Laudato Si'*: On Care for Our Common Home." Vatican City: Libreria Editrice Vaticana, 2015. laudatosi.com.

Rhodium Group. "Preliminary US Emissions Estimates for 2018." January 8, 2019. rhg.com/research/preliminary-us-emissions-estimates-for-2018/.

Rockström, Johan, Owen Gaffney, Joeri Rogelj, Malte Meinshausen, Nebojsa Nakicenovic, and Hans Joachim Schellnhuber. "A Roadmap for Rapid Decarbonization." *Science* 355, no. 6331 (March 2017): 1269–71. doi.org/10.1126/science.aah3443.

Rogelj, Joeri, Drew Shindell, Kejun Jiang, Solomone Fifita, Piers Forster, Veronika Ginzburg, Collins Handa, et al. "Mitigation Pathways Compatible with 1.5°C in the Context of Sustainable Development." In *Global Warming of 1.5°C: An IPCC Special Report on the Impacts of Global Warming of 1.5°C Above Pre-Industrial Levels and Related*

Global Greenhouse Gas Emission Pathways in the Context of Strengthening the Global Response to the Threat of Climate Change, Sustainable Development, and Efforts to Eradicate Poverty, edited by V. Masson-Delmotte, P. Zhai, H. O. Pörtner, D. Roberts, J. Skea, P. R. Shukla, A. Pirani, et al., 93–174. Geneva: The Intergovernmental Panel on Climate Change (IPCC), October 9, 2018. ipcc.ch/site/assets/uploads/sites/2/2019/02/SR15_Chapter2_Low_Res.pdf.

Roser, Max, and Hannah Ritchie. "Food per Person." 2017. ourworldindata.org/food-per-person.

Rotz, Sarah. "'They Took Our Beads, It Was a Fair Trade, Get Over It': Settler Colonial Logics, Racial Hierarchies and Material Dominance in Canadian Agriculture." *Geoforum* 82 (June 2017): 158–69. doi.org/10.1016/j.geoforum.2017.04.010.

Rowe, Stan. *Home Place*. Edmonton: NeWest Press, 1992.

Roy, Eleanor Ainge. "New Zealand River Granted Same Legal Rights as Human Being." *Guardian*, March 16, 2017. theguardian.com/world/2017/mar/16/new-zealand-river-granted-same-legal-rights-as-human-being.

Sánchez-Bayo, Francisco, and Kris A. G. Wyckhuys. "Worldwide Decline of the Entomofauna: A Review of Its Drivers." *Biological Conservation* 232 (April 2019): 8–27. doi.org/10.1016/j.biocon.2019.01.020.

Saul, John Ralston. *A Fair Country: Telling Truths About Canada*. Toronto: Viking Canada, 2008.

Saunders, Doug. "Getting Ready for a No-Growth Future." *Globe and Mail*, January 5, 2008.

Senate Standing Committee on Agriculture and Forestry. "Feast or Famine: Impacts of Climate Change and Carbon Pricing on Agriculture, Agri-Food and Forestry." Ottawa: Senate of Canada, 2018.

Seufert, Verena, and Navin Ramankutty. "Many Shades of Gray — The Context-Dependent Performance of Organic Agriculture." *Science Advances* 3, no. 3 (2017). advances. sciencemag.org/content/3/3/e1602638.full.

Sigurdsson, Valdimar, Nils Magne Larsen, and Didrik Gunnarsson. "An In-Store Experimental Analysis of Consumers' Selection of Fruits and Vegetables." *The Service Industries Journal* 31, no. 15 (December 2010): 2587–2602. doi.org/10.1080/02642069.2011.531126.

Smil, Vaclav. *Feeding the World: A Challenge for the 21st Century.* Cambridge, MA: MIT Press, 2000.

Stanley, Paige L., Jason E. Rowntree, David K. Beede, Marcia S. DeLonge, and Michael W. Hamm. "Impacts of Soil Carbon Sequestration on Life Cycle Greenhouse Gas Emissions in Midwestern USA Beef Finishing Systems." *Agricultural Systems* 162 (May 2018): 249–58. doi.org/10.1016/j. agsy.2018.02.003.

Statista. "Consumption of Frozen Fries in Canada from 2009 to 2016." 2018. statista.com/statistics/448685/ frozen-fries-consumption-in-canada/.

Steffen, Will, Katherine Richardson, Johan Rockström, Sarah E. Cornell, Ingo Fetzer, Elena M. Bennett, Reinette Biggs, et al. "Planetary Boundaries: Guiding Human Development on a Changing Planet." *Science* 347, no. 6223 (February 2015). doi.org/10.1126/ science.1259855.

Steffen, Will, Johan Rockström, Katherine Richardson, Timothy M. Lenton, Carl Folke, Diana Liverman, Colin

P. Summerhayes, et al. "Trajectories of the Earth System in the Anthropocene." *PNAS* 115, no. 33 (August 2018): 8252–59. doi.org/10.1073/pnas.1810141115.

Stiglitz, Joseph. *Globalization and Its Discontents*. London: W. W. Norton, 2003.

Tarasuk, Valerie, Joyce Cheng, Claire de Oliveira, Naomi Dachner, Craig Gundersen, and Paul Kurdyak. "Association Between Household Food Insecurity and Annual Health Care Costs." *CMAJ* 187, no. 14 (October 2015). doi.org/10.1503/cmaj.150234.

Teasdale, John R., Charles B. Coffman, and Ruth W. Mangum. "Potential Long-Term Benefits of No Tillage and Organic Cropping Systems for Grain Production and Soil Improvement." *Agronomy Journal* 99 (September–October 2007): 1297–1305. doi.org/10.2134/agronj2006.0362.

Teilhard de Chardin, Pierre. *The Phenomenon of Man*. London: Collins Fontana Books, 1972.

Tertzakian, Peter. "100 Million Barrels a Day — This Time the Oil Boom Really Is Different." *Financial Post*, September 4, 2018. business.financialpost.com/commodities/energy/peter-tertzakian-this-time-the-global-oil-boom-really-is-different.

Twist, Lynne. *The Soul of Money: Reclaiming the Wealth of Our Inner Resources*. New York: W. W. Norton, 2003.

Umeh, Kanayo, and Maxine Sharps. "Psychological Requirements for Increased Fruit and Vegetable Intake in Young Adults." *British Food Journal* 114, no. 9 (2012): 1310–24. doi.org/10.1108/00070701211258844.

Walton, Alice G. "The Unfortunate Health Risks of French Fries." *Forbes*, June 14, 2017. forbes.com/sites/

alicegwalton/2017/06/14/the-unfortunate-health-risks-of-french-fries/#2c9fb59d1bdf.

Wartman, Paul, Kari E. Dunfield, Kamini Khosla, Cora Loucks, Rene Van Acker, and Ralph C. Martin. "The Establishment of Apple Orchards as Temperate Forest Garden Systems and Their Impact on Indigenous Bacterial and Fungal Population Abundance in Southern Ontario, Canada." *Renewable Agriculture and Food Systems* 332, no. 2 (April 2017): 157–68. doi.org/10.1017/S1742170516000120.

Wartman, Paul, Rene Van Acker, and Ralph C. Martin. "Temperate Agroforestry: How Forest Garden Systems Combined with People-Based Ethics Can Transform Culture." *Sustainability* 10, no. 7 (June 2018): 2246. doi.org/10.3390/su10072246.

Watts, Jonathan. "We Have 12 Years to Limit Climate Change Catastrophe, Warns UN." *Guardian*, October 8, 2018. theguardian.com/environment/2018/oct/08/global-warming-must-not-exceed-15c-warns-landmark-un-report?utm_term=R3VhcmRpYW4gVG9kYYXkgVUstMT-gxMDA4&utm_source=esp&um_medium=Email&utm_campaign=GuardianTodayUK&CMP=GTUK_email.

Weingarten, Marc. "Home Alone: How Living in Too Large a House Almost Destroyed My Marriage." *Globe and Mail*, July 28, 2018. theglobeandmail.com/opinion/article-living-in-too-large-a-house-almost-destroyed-our-marriage/.

Whitehead, Ross D., Gozde Ozakinci, Ian D. Stephen, and David I. Perrett. "Appealing to Vanity: Could Potential Appearance Improvement Motivate Fruit and Vegetable Consumption?" *American Journal of Public Health* 102, no. 2 (February 2012): 207–11.

Willett, Walter, Johan Rockström, Brent Loken, Marco Springmann, Tim Lang, Sonja Vermeulen, Tara Garnett, et al. "Food in the Anthropocene: The EAT–*Lancet* Commission on Healthy Diets from Sustainable Food Systems." *The Lancet* 393, no. 10170 (February 2019): 447–92. doi.org/10.1016/S0140-6736(18)31788-4.

Wilson, E. O. *The Creation: An Appeal to Save Life on Earth.* New York: W. W. Norton & Company, 2007.

Wiltshire, Andrew. "Implications of Climate Change for Agricultural Productivity in the Early Twenty-First Century." *Philosophical Transactions of the Royal Society B: Biological Sciences* 365, no. 1554 (September 2010): 2973–89. royalsocietypublishing.org/doi/10.1098/rstb.2010.0158.

Woods, Jeremy, Adrian Williams, John K. Hughes, Mairi Black, and Richard Murphy. "Energy and the Food System." *Philosophical Transactions of the Royal Society B: Biological Sciences* 365, no. 1554 (September 2010): 2991–3006. doi.org/10.1098/rstb.2010.0172.

Yale Rudd Center for Food Policy & Obesity. "Youth-Focused Food Marketing: Examining the Spending Trends." New Haven, CT: Yale Rudd Center for Food Policy and Obesity, 2013. bridgingthegapresearch.org/_asset/4z16fw/BTG-Rudd-Food-Marketing-brief_FINAL.pdf.